The Journey "Home"

Choices In Life and with God

**By Dr. Sandra Didenko Varney and
Moise Ndjomou**

The Journey "Home": Choices in Life and with God.
By Dr. Sandra Didenko Varney and Moise Ndjomou

Copyright ©2025 Dr. Sandra Didenko Varney and Moise Ndjomou.

ISBN: 978-1-938283-46-8

Published by Writing Career Coach Press. Toledo, OH.

1.Memoir. 2.Christian Living. 3.History/World War II

Forward
By Bob Varney

This is a story of three generations of a family caught in circumstances beyond their control, where God continually intervened. His grace and mercy are seen throughout these generations. The story is told by my wife Sandra Varney from the stories that were experienced and passed along in her family. Many were passed along verbally like the accounts written in the Bible; some were written in memoires.

The story begins some time after the end of Tsar Nicholas' rule of Russia. His regime was overthrown during the Bolshevik Revolution and Communism was brought into that region. The story centers on a specific Ukrainian family -- the Didenko family. It traces their lives over three generations from 1918 to 2018. The story starts with a midnight raid followed by execution of Sandra's grandfather. It continues with a tumultuous multi-year journey traveling across Europe in a covered wagon, living in a refugee camp and ending in America, the land of opportunity for those who value family, hard work, and helping others who are less fortunate. It's a heart-warming, though traumatic, story of God's grace, provision, and blessings.

The story is supplemented with spiritual observations by Moise Ndjomou *(MN),* and myself *(RCV)*. The spiritual observations are in italics so they are easily recognizable. This multiple-author experience allows the reader to hear an amazing story firsthand and then pause to reflect on mankind. Together, *The Journey Home* with these reflections, paints a rich picture of life ---- how it is, how it ought to be and some encouragement for redeeming actions in similar circumstances today toward ways where God's kingdom on earth can function well and honor God.

Dedication
By Sandra Varney

I want to dedicate this book to my father Yuri (George) Didenko for a life well lived through both trials and victories. For me, he was an example of the "salt of the earth" good values and hard work leading to achievement, and a role model of a glass always half full, when it comes to contentment in life no matter what you encounter in the journey.

Acknowledgements
By Sandra Varney

I want to thank all the people who listened to my story and encouraged me to write a book. Fifteen years of false writing starts and three consuming years of serious writing later, the dream of "The Book" is a reality.

Thank you to my sweet husband and soul mate, who was always there encouraging me through all the highs and lows. I thank my family who participated in the journey, especially my youngest daughter Karlayne Powars, who designed the cover.

Finally, I am thankful for Cyndi G. Wagner, who is a delightful part of our family and was the editor of the book, contributing invaluable changes to the writing flow of the story

Table of Contents

Part 1: The Name

The Journey Home
Choices In Life and with God

God said in the book of Habakkuk, the vision is for an appointed time. Though it tarry, wait for it. We will keep moving forward and God will make something beautiful.

Chapter 1 - The Story Behind the Name

The weather was so beautiful on that day! I almost sensed something wonderful was about to happen. The sky was blue with warm sunshine filling the room. With a nice breeze on my skin, I was sitting in a Leadership Master class in Mazatlán Mexico, waiting for the next speaker to be introduced. Suddenly, I heard the voice of Mr. David Hamilton introducing Dr. Bob and his wife Dr. Sandra as our speakers. To my surprise, Bob's topic on The Divine Conductor began with the story about Sandra. Right at the beginning as she started telling Her Story, my attention was no longer on the nice breeze on my skin. There was a convincing anointed atmosphere full of grace and lessons to be learned from her story in the room! At one point, I heard a voice telling me that the story of this woman should be written in a book because many people will learn about the ways of God and His works as they read it. Although Sandra was presenting a story of her life starting with her father's life, her story was not at all about her or about her father but it was about her Heavenly Father, the Creator of the universe

3

making a way in the wilderness and guiding the steps of ordinary people. As you read this story, I hope there are things you will learn that will challenge you to listen and to obey God more than ever before. **(MN)**

Dr. Sandra Varney begins Her Story.

While this is a story that spans three generations, I really feel it is my father's story rather than mine because it started with the stories that he told me in my childhood. It includes me because I experienced the trials of a refugee life, the challenges of being an immigrant child and the joy of becoming a naturalized citizen. As an immigrant living in an adopted country, America means something deeply different to me than it does to a person who was born here.

My father has a lot to do with my deep love for this country. My father arrived in America as a man with two suitcases, a sick wife, and a young child. I was four and a half years old. He was forty years old and neither of us spoke a word of English. However, he arrived here propelled by powerful drive to survive and a deep loyalty to his family name. As for me, I was just growing up in a family and navigating an immigrant life style that I knew was quite different from that of people around me.

I am in the winter season of my life so I have told my story many times to many people. Through the years of storytelling, I acquired a growing understanding of what my parents lived through, how God miraculously continued to provide for them, and for my father's drive and tenacious loyalty to his family name. However most

4

of all, with every telling of the story, I grew in my love and indebtedness for this country. I gained an appreciation for the core values entrenched in America's culture. With each story, I grew in my gratefulness for the generous heart and genuine willingness of the American people to embrace those less fortunate than they with a helping hand. It is worth pausing to say that Americans stand out as a people with a strong will, an innovative mind, a gentle spirit and most of all a kind generous heart. You, as Americans, need to occasionally be reminded of that and applauded. This book is written as a thank you to my adopted country and my friends. It is written so that my children and grandchildren NEVER forget to be proud of who they are, and are forever grateful for where they live…in the Land of the free and the Home of the brave. It is a rare gift to be treasured in each of our hearts.

By the time my father arrived in America, he had already overcome so much. While he had ambition, my father realized he couldn't pursue personal dreams while simultaneously taking care of his family. Whatever feelings of ambition were in his heart, he just transplanted them into this four and a half year old little girl standing at his side and here I am reflecting back! I truly believe that I am the poster child for America, and what you can achieve in this Land of Opportunity. During my childhood, the American people with their big hearts willingly embraced anybody who they saw working hard to attain their dreams.

Listening to this part of Sandra's story, it is obviously clear that, the way a nation or a community welcomes, loves, protects and takes care of strangers (or not), tells you if there are biblical values in their cultural foundation (or not). Love for a stranger does not naturally abide inside a human heart. It originates and is planted there from God. That kind of love allows everyone from any culture or language to dream and to have the opportunity to blossom! **(MN)**

This Land of Opportunity and its love for strangers is in stark contrast to life in Ukraine under autocratic rule. Growing up, I never was confused about who were the good people and who were the bad. The endless stories which my father would tell at the dinner table on special occasions, kept my two sisters and me glued to our seats and became emblazed in our little minds forever. My father lived during the Bolshevik Revolution into communism and through WWII as a young man. His experiences in those formative adult years established some key core values that framed how he then chose to live out the rest of his life and thus they continue to frame how I live out my life today.

Unfortunately, many people don't know the detailed truth of what happened during the Bolshevik revolution --- the effects of the aftermath that it had on the world stage forever, and the impact it continues to have on people living in Ukraine. Much of the atrocities were suppressed or ignored for the benefit of strongly rooting the autocratic communist philosophy into the Soviet Union culture and to accommodate modern-day political dynamics at that time on the world stage.

Chapter 2 - Russian History as it Relates to Ukraine

I know not everyone likes history. However, every nation has a history that tells you if the leaders and the people were building a culture of freedom, justice, and generosity according to the Creator of the universe. A nation's history can also tell you if the foundation of that nation was built on oppression, injustice, and abuse. I hope you know the history of your nation. Let's learn a little about what happened between Russia and Ukraine. **(MN)**

It is important to first understand a little about Russian history and how it intertwined with Ukraine's history leading to the Bolshevik Revolution of 1917. This event changed the political landscape, not only in Russia and Eastern Europe; but actually, changed how history would play out for the whole world from that day forth.

For centuries, the Russian Empire, which often included Ukraine, practiced serfdom as their economic model. Serfdom was a form of feudalism where landless peasants served the landowning nobility. In the serfdom era, small village estates, each owned by a single wealthy peasant family, dotted the countryside of Ukraine. The rich peasant farmers who owned land hired landless peasants to work the estate farms in exchange for housing, food and small wages. While this practice mostly ended in the Middle Ages, it continued in Russia well into the early 1900's because significant portions of Russia and most of Ukraine were economically dependent on agriculture and rural in nature.

Ukraine especially had rich black soil and ideal weather conditions for farming grains, corn, and sunflowers. The most fertile soil found around the world is called "black super soil" or Chernozem. One quarter of this soil is located in the country of Ukraine. As a nation, Ukraine can provide food for half a billion people and is the fifth largest grain producer in the world. Along with Russia, it provides a quarter of the global wheat production.

In the late 1800's, Russia was an impoverished nation with an enormous population of peasant people and a fast-growing minority of poor industrial workers. When industrialization finally reached that area of the world in the 1900's, it created even more economic disparity and led to immense social and political unrest. Populations in major Russian cities doubled, resulting in overcrowded and destitute living conditions for the industrial city workers. The farm workers in the rural areas of the country joined the growing wave of dissatisfaction among the working class. At the time, the monarchy was headed by Czar Nicholas II who was not gifted with strong leadership skills.

To appease the unrest, Czar Nicholas II reluctantly set up a representative branch of government called the Imperial State Duma in 1905. However, the Duma diminished to a puppet role in the government instead of actually governing the people. For the next 10 years, the demands for social reform kept increasing and giving a stronger voice to the Bolsheviks and other revolutionary groups supporting extreme socialist political values. A series of poor diplomatic and economic decisions by Czar Nicholas II fueled the flames of unrest even further. Finally, in March 1917, huge crowds of demonstrators clamored for bread and took to the streets in Petrograd (presently St. Petersburg.) The army, which was sent to squelch the riot, joined the striking workers and peasants instead, forcing Czar Nicholas II to abdicate the throne. The whole royal family was placed under house arrest in a private residence before being executed a year later.

Duma immediately formed a provisional government assembled from leaders of the bourgeois capitalist class. Their constitution was based on free speech, equality before the law and the right to organize using quiet reforms rather than social revolution. Unfortunately, the increasing food supply problems, and the poor living conditions only added to an increasing unrest which continued to fuel the growing socialist revolutionary movement. By fall of that year, the leftist political revolutionaries had grown in power sufficiently that the Bolshevik Party leader Vladimir Lenin led a quick almost bloodless coup and overthrew both the Duma and the Russian provisional government. They then formed a new government that was to be ruled directly by the military, peasants, and workers based on Marxism; and led by Lenin. Thus, the world's first communist country was birthed with Vladimir Lenin as its dictator.

With the chaotic overthrow of Czar Nicholas II and the explosive disorganization of the Bolsheviks, Ukraine seized the opportunity to declare itself an independent country with its own government in 1918. Soon after this bold move, the newly formed Ukraine republic had to face a monumental challenge of being at war simultaneously with dual aggressors Russia and Poland. Both of these countries were looking for a much-needed source of food for their hunger-plagued people. After a failed treaty attempt to align itself with Poland, Ukraine was unable to withstand the continued onslaughts from the Russian army any longer. Ukraine, known as the Breadbasket of Europe, was annexed as a republic of USSR and became the Bread Basket of Russia in 1922. (A hundred years later, history seems to be repeating itself with Russia once more intentionally invading Ukraine in February 2022.)

Although the toppling of the Duma government was simple and straight forward, maintaining control of power by the Bolshevik Party was far harder and more complex. These were tumultuous times as guerrilla resistance against the Bolshevik regime clandestinely formed by a loose alliance of supporters (White Army) who wanted a more democratic style of socialism. They continued to spawn political instability in the country for almost 5 years before the Bolshevik Red Army declared victory in 1923. With rising Ukrainian nationalism and guerilla resistance continuing to be especially strong, Lenin and his younger rising cohort Joseph Stalin decided that the Soviet Union republics had to be more tightly held under the rule of a strong centralized Russian government even if it meant greater oppression of the people to achieve it. The communist government in Moscow assumed all authority over foreign relations, military, and commerce. Paramount oppressive authority was exercised at all levels of government in the constituent republics of the Soviet Union.

This new Bolshevik's Communist Regime had two formidable challenges: **First**, to rebuild the economy. **Second**, to consolidate the non-Russian nationalities into a centralized Russian toned culture.

These challenges were aggressively implemented on two parallel tracks:

1. Nationalization of all enterprises, both agricultural and industrial, was called collectivization. It meant immediate expropriation of all privately-owned land as well as swift initiation of government control over all industrialization throughout all of the Soviet Union republics.
2. Penetration of the non-Russian nationalities like Ukraine with Russian traditions, literature, and

language was implemented throughout all spheres of that society with intent to eradicate their cultural identity and to assimilate them into the Russian culture.

It was #1 that led to my father's family's demise:

By the time Lenin died in 1924, Joseph Stalin was well positioned to take his place as leader of the ruling Communist Party and of the whole Soviet Union. Stalin immediately launched his first 5 Year Plan initiating breakneck industrialization throughout all of the Soviet Union. In the Ukraine, that translated into completing national collectivization of all farm land by confiscating all privately-owned property. The brunt of this burden was borne by the rich peasant landowners whom the Russians called Kulaks. The Russian regime labelled Kulaks as "enemies of the Soviet State and the common people"; and thus by definition needed to be eliminated as a people group by the Soviet government in order to facilitate the state's agenda of expropriation of farmland into state owned-collective farms. In the late 1920's, at the height of the collectivization program, almost two million of these people were either executed or deported to Siberia and the Far North. Some 100,000 families were torn apart and many were deported to settlements in Siberia as their new home.

Chapter 3 – Back to My Story

My grandfather was one of those wealthy landowners that the central Russian government described as ruthless, unkind, and selfish. My father's family was labelled as Kulaks and the fate of the whole family and their future was irreversibly and permanently changed. Contrary to the Russian label, I discovered personally that my grandfather was a kind and generous landowner. In 1994 when we visited the very land that my grandfather owned, we met some families whose ancestors had worked on my grandfather's farm. For generations the Ukrainian families who lived and worked the land there, revered the Didenko name. One woman that we met on the street told us that she remembered as a child that whenever an argument erupted, her parents or grandparents would intervene to stop it by reminding everyone that their arguing while standing on this land was bringing unrest to Didenko's soul and trampling his spirit.

The easiest plan for the Moscow government regime to facilitate the expropriation of land was to have the Bolsheviks unexpectedly ride into the village on horseback in the middle of the night. This sudden random event was used to create a dual surprise effect of fear and shock. They went to the rich landowner's house and arrested any male eighteen and older. Then they took all the women and children under 18 and put them into the poorest peasants' homes; and opened up the landowner's house to all the peasant field workers and their families.

You can imagine the chaos that ensued. As the wealthy family, you helplessly watched in horror as everything you owned was plundered by villagers whom you had cared for faithfully for years. If you had been a kind and fair employer, it had to be emotionally wrenching, confusing, and devastating. You saw the worst of human nature come out when left to its own by excluding God and His Spirit from the picture of life. These village families that you knew and kindly cared for through the years were now joining Bolshevik outsiders to plunder and destroy everything you owned. It was human nature displayed at its lowest mundane level of greed and selfishness.

What happens in a nation when people begin to steal what is not theirs in order to become rich, thinking that they will have an easier life? What happens when a government abuses its power to create a platform where families can be abused? Well, do you remember the story of Naboth in the Holy Scriptures?

In I Kings 21, there is a similar story. The government's leaders abused Naboth and killed him, because they wanted his family's land. Ahab, who was King of Samaria at the time, had a lot of land and power; but he was not satisfied! Ahab coveted the vineyard of his neighbor, Naboth. Naboth refused to give Ahab the vineyard which was the inheritance from Naboth's father. Queen Jezebel, the wife of Ahab and the daughter of the King of Sidon, orchestrated the death of Naboth. He was stoned to death and his vineyard was seized because of greed (I Kings 21:1-29). Ahab's story and how God punished him and his family continues to be a warning today for all those who are still under the power of greed.

Many things can lead people to greed; and subsequently, greed can lead people to many disasters. Some aspects of life that lead to greed are: selfishness, pride, materialism, idolatry, love of money, ungratefulness, dissatisfaction and the lack of a fear of God. Greed causes people to do many ugly things: to steal, to kill, to abuse, to be sexually immoral, to divorce, and to hide from God. When greed is present in people's hearts, they want everything only for themselves. Appreciating others and celebrating the victories of others gradually becomes harder and harder.

*Greed is dangerous because it breaks relationships and destroys people's lives. Greed is based on selfishness and it actually creates poverty and injustice. These bad results did not only happen with Ahab or the Bolsheviks, but it can be seen today… in families, in communities, in nations! Turning away from God's love, His justice, and His mercy is an open invitation for greed to take place. **(MN)***

Sandra continued Her Story!

In my father's village, his family was that rich landowner who lived on a big estate and their farming operation provided the livelihood for most of the villagers. It also meant that they were the central target when the Bolsheviks arrived in the late hours of the night to uproot the landowner system of life and disrupt the whole village. As the oldest son, and over 18, my father was arrested and taken to prison with his father while the rest of the family was evicted onto the street.

Even as a child, I wondered many times what it must have been like for my father. As I moved through life, first when I turned eighteen, then as a mother myself, and then the mother of children turning eighteen, I pondered how I would have responded if I were in my father's position, or as my grandmother—or even as my grandfather? They lived in a world without farm equipment, cars, airplanes, electricity, television, cell telephones or internet. Their life was one of simply farming the land, regulated by sunrises and sunsets…plus seasonal changes during the year.

Putting yourself into this picture, you can imagine the simple living pattern of family landowners and villagers that had continued for generations previously. Then, you can imagine hearing the rumors of the Czar and his family being executed. You know there is a civil war but it has not affected your village. You hope against hope for eventual resolution and peace in the country not ever imagining the incomprehensible. Peace does not seem like it is coming. You may sense the approach of new changes on the horizon; but in the big picture of life, you feel quite small/insignificant in the world. You certainly feel helpless to stop and try to affect anything on the national stage. And then, one night you hear a lot of noise, clamor and loud voices at your door and your whole world turns upside down where nothing makes sense anymore. The family farm, passed from generation to generation, that you grew up on…the comfort of your home, the warmth and love of your family …is snatched from you with your life never to be the same again. You are dragged away from your family to an unknown fate. You watch your mother and siblings left behind, sobbing, huddled in the darkness. You are seething with fear and anger but powerless to do anything.

I simply cannot imagine the strength and personal resilience it took for my grandfather and father to survive, let alone gather up the will strength and to push forward with life.

Both my father and grandfather were taken to the same prison but were segregated in different sections for younger men and older men. The younger men were assigned jobs around the prison grounds while the older men were kept in their cells awaiting their fate. At times my father's errands or duties would bring him past his father's cell and they would sneak a short opportunity to talk; but in actuality there was very little to say when your heart is filled with hopelessness. The young men supported each other emotionally as best they could while dealing with a future filled with fears of the unknown.

My father's cell mate often had daily assignments to process paperwork in the main office. One evening when he returned to the cell, he said, "Yura, I am so sorry. Your father is on the list for tomorrow night."

Everyone knew about "the list". It was the list of names of men scheduled to be executed. At eighteen years of age, my father had the challenge to set his grief aside temporarily; and figure out how to see his father one last time. He could not risk his cell mate's safety for divulging the information. However, he had to find a way to share this devasting news of the coming execution with his father so they could say their last goodbyes.

My father was not going to miss the opportunity to say a final goodbye to his father. He managed to somehow find a way to go past his father's cell. I have wondered for the better part of my life what their exchange must have been like and the emotional strength my father had to find in order to complete such a momentous task at such a young age. He could not show any real emotion as it could tip off the guards that my father knew something about what was going to happen. With God's help, he was able to hold strong emotionally, find an opportunity to walk past my grandfather's cell, take his hand and say.

"You are on the list for tonight, Dad."

Can you imagine being able to say that sentence to your own father? Someone you looked up to and loved your whole life. Someone who has raised you from birth and was there for you in every childhood challenge that came your way. But then I also think of my grandfather having to hear this from his oldest son and stay strong emotionally. Sometimes in the context of history we forget these were real people with real emotions. If you have children, stop for a moment and think of all the emotions you would feel if your child had to inform you that you had hours left here on the earth. You had to prepare to enter eternity. You would never see your spouse or any of your children again. There was nothing you could do to take care of them, provide for them or protect them. You could NOT even hug your first born son who was standing in front of you with iron bars separating the two of you. You could not promise that everything would be alright because you did not know the future; and even worse, if you were to guess, you knew the future most likely was going to be dark and unpredictable. Life would never be the same again as it had been.

I cannot imagine emotionally navigating such an unfathomable situation. My children are fully grown and successful, happy middle-aged adults. My father was barely an adult when this tragedy in life was thrust upon him. My grandfather had three children under 19 years old. He probably was looking forward to a full abundant life watching them grow up and having grandchildren, while he aged slowly into the silver years of his life. That is what had historically happened to his ancestors in generations past. The horrors and life altering atrocities that one human being with the force of the government behind him can inflict on another is still hard for me to comprehend on most days. That is why we all need God to be in us and with us. We all need a Savior.

I have heard my father's story many, many times. Parts of it will continue to be an emotional mystery to me even as I take my last breath. When I was about eighteen, my father's age when he was put in prison, picturing the gravity of his story had an even more profound impact on me. Can you imagine having to say goodbye for the last time to your own father? How would you survive? The sobriety of those thoughts really sunk deep into my soul. I had been trying to honor my father as well as joining him in wanting to fulfill all the dreams he had for my life...all the dreams that he had to give up in his own life's journey. I wondered how I would have reacted to these kinds of circumstances. I always came up short except for one sole comforting thought. "If God ever required that of me in my life then He would walk beside me and it would have to be His strength NOT mine to accomplish it. I rest confidently in His promises that He would do just that."

The question that I did ask most often of my father was, "What did you say to each other in those last moments saying good-bye?" His answer was always the same. Sometimes with a tear in his eye, he would say, "Honey, What was left to say? We quietly cried a little. Brushing tears off our cheeks, we hugged through the prison bars. Then shook hands and with a final whispered good bye ... I walked away."

My father always finished that part of the story the same way. "At around midnight they were all awakened to yelling and loud noises of people being herded and corralled. They heard sounds that people create when they're being shoved and prodded along -- loud voices, scuffing shoes, shuffling feet, sounds of stumbling; and then distant voices and noises echoing in the courtyard and then the execution."

And then, that was it… silence.

After listening to this section of Sandy's story, many people are deeply moved and cry from their heart, "Why? That was not fair, that was not just!" At this point, it is obvious that if a government practices injustice, it will be using its power to oppress, steal people's freedom, and kill their future.

This story is painful to digest, a father unjustly condemned for execution and a son forced to declare that his father was an enemy of the state, basically renouncing his family heritage and name. It shows how the wickedness of leaders is always exposed not only by what they believe, but through their actions. The fact that both men were not executed is a miracle! It shows that God was somehow making a way to fulfill the plan that he still had for Sandra's father. It is easy to imagine the absence of God when the wickedness of mankind seems to prevail with such strength. Those who have faith in the Creator of the Universe can still see His presence in the midst of the worst of storms and unimaginable injustice. He is God and He is omnipresent.

The Holy Scriptures describe Jesus as "despised and rejected—a man of sorrows, acquainted with deepest grief. We turned our backs on him and looked the other way. He was despised, and we did not care." (Isaiah 53:3). The Messiah's situation was worse than being a kulak, or in a communist prison. His situation was worse than any situation you can ever imagine for one purpose. Jesus Christ accepted all that rejection and humiliation so that you can realize how much He loves you and that you will make a choice to have a relationship with Him. It will be interesting to read further in this story how Sandra's father discovered that and surrendered his life to Him for eternity. **(MN)**

Sandra continued Her Story…about further challenges facing her father!

My father, at eighteen at that moment in 1927, became the eldest male of the Didenko household with the responsibility of caring for family members landing on his young shoulders. He had a mother, a younger brother and sister. All of them were still alive somewhere BUT he was still in prison. For my father, now as the head of his household, the world that he had known crashed and burned around him, due to no fault of his own. There was only one choice before him. The only way to care for the living was to betray the dead. He had to get out of prison!

The only way to survive…to get out of prison… was to declare that his father was an enemy of the state, deny his family name and heritage, and furthermore embrace the philosophy of communism i.e. all property was government owned and equality of the working class. This had become the foundation of the Russian regime, He was required to sign a document saying that his father was a Kulak, an enemy of the government and the common people. He personally had to reject the family name and wholeheartedly support the ruling communist regime that pretended to stand for equality to the common people and laborers. Furthermore, he had to renounce all his father's beliefs about God, free enterprise, integrity, hard work and many of the biblical values that he had been raised on. This was the very belief system that my father grew up with and watched his father live out as father and young son farmed together on their estate. These beliefs had become the core of my father's personal values.

A person born of a Kulak family could only escape the Bolshevik imprisonment and gain freedom by signing a paper denying his family's name. Essentially, the individual had to support his relative's execution by agreeing that his relative had been "an enemy of the state." This declaration made by government edict was a strategy to destroy the bourgeois class and give "power of rule to the people". (This all sounded like initial beginnings of democracy; but it was so far from that.)

Today people don't place as much weight on the importance of a person's family name and their honor, but for my father's and grandfather's generations—and mine as well—a person's name was their reputation wrapped in their identity. You guarded your reputation and you wanted to reflect well on your family. Your handshake was as strong and trusted as a signed, notarized contract today. To deny your family was a cruel and family destructive requirement. It was part of the strategy that the Bolsheviks used to force loyalty to the state —over God or family. They rejected the very idea of a Supreme Being, let alone a God who loved you enough to sacrifice His life for you. They replaced it with human atheism. They pitted children against parents—telling children that their parents were not as enlightened as their own young minds and that it was their patriotic duty to report their parents to the authorities if they saw them straying from the beliefs and philosophy of the communist state and the working-class philosophy.

From a different perspective there is another question that is worthy of some deep reflection. What happens when one sphere of society takes advantage and abuses another sphere? Another way to ask this question is "What will happen if one sphere of influence like government exceeds its authority and trespasses onto the authority of another sphere, for instance, family? The simple answer: there will be chaos and injustice.

God revealed to Loren Cunningham, the founder of Youth with a Mission, that in every society there are seven spheres of influence: Government, Family, Education, Religion, Economy (Business, Science and Technology), Celebration (Arts and Entertainment), and Media. Those spheres of influence have the same value before God but play different roles. Today, as in the days of the Bolsheviks, some governments are exerting their authority over families, in education, or in science and technology. If a government used its power to force Education to teach that God does not exist or in any way disallow the Religion sphere the freedom to teach religious concepts, they are leading the nation astray.

Reflection: What injustices are people observing among the different spheres of the society where you live and can you suggest solutions to bring back order? What needs to be done when the government puts innocent, powerless, and guiltless people in prison or kills them? As you begin to reflect deeply on these questions, it is good to continue to read the story. It's worth pondering how acts of injustice cause brokenness and pain, but also how God's redemption can make a way where there seems to be NO way! **(MN)**

It was clear to my father that his fate would be no different than his father's fate in prison, unless he signed the document. So he did sign it under great duress, asking both his father and God to forgive him. My father was let out of prison in 1929 right after he turned 20 years old. However, he still was not completely a free man. He was required to carry an ID card stating that he came from a Kulak family and that his father had been executed as an enemy of the state. My father had to show the card when applying for work and on other specified occasions. It was a type of branding similar to a criminal record in today's culture. The ID card definitely impacted your job opportunities and career mobility in a strong negative way.

Kulak families were treated poorly by almost everyone, almost as a social trend. It was a society based on fear where no one trusted anyone else, not parent and child, not husband and wife, not friend to friend or neighbor to neighbor, and certainly not employer to employee. So, while he signed the official document to gain his freedom, my father was still compromised in gaining access to many life's opportunities and navigating life successfully. He pondered this reality for a few days; and then quietly, in the privacy of his room, he chose to tear up the card and take his chances on navigating his new life without it rather than allowing himself to be labelled unfairly. He told us that this card was too painful a reminder of the warm loving family life he had known and what had become of his family.

For years he survived by constantly staying on the move with different jobs. He was especially motivated as he had to find ways to support his mother and two younger siblings who were living in abject poverty. In the years that followed, he would consistently leave money, food staples and supplies in designated various areas in the woods for his family to later pick up. It was a means of survival for all of them until the living conditions under Russian rule became more stable.

My father was an amazing man with an engaging personality that immediately put you at ease when you met him. His handsome appearance and 6'2 build made him noticeable; but it was his engaging, down to earth, easy going personality that drew you to him. He also had a very serious side to him that quickly converted into a pragmatic survival instinct when needed. That continued to serve him well when necessary. I was in my sixties when my father died and it was a surprisingly monumental loss in my life and my two sisters' lives.

We never knew anybody who did not like our father the minute they met him nor did not enjoy his company. He was a hard-working man. A generous, social person by nature, he enjoyed life and being happy. He had a way of making you feel good about yourself and about all of life when you were around him. At first meeting, he immediately could engage a person to feel warm and valued by his conversation. Watching from the sidelines. you would think he never met a stranger. He always saw abundance and blessings in whatever circumstances life happened to give him; many of which an ordinary person would not have welcomed to experience. For him the glass was always half full and there was plenty of apples on the tree for everyone to get their full share. There was a generous kindness about him that allowed him to help many people in need whenever he could without any expectation of acknowledgement on their part for what he did.

My suspicion is that he was happy by nature and I attribute the flourishing of that feeling to the warm loving family environment that God provided him in his childhood. He never lost faith in God, confidence in himself, and the belief of being abundantly rich in life's blessings no matter what circumstances beset him.

I think that attitude served him well as a young man experiencing waves of horrific emotions in prison. It helped him survive twenty plus years under communist rule as he secretly supported his family while moving up the ranks in various jobs. It sustained him with the courage to navigate the challenging, dangerous journey on the war front; and to face the uncertain future in an unfamiliar country carrying the responsibility of a wife and child on his shoulders. At forty years old, he had to start a new life in an unfamiliar country with no familiar cultural foundation from his past to help him.

Chapter 4 – Surviving Professional Life under Communism

I wonder what some people would choose today if they had to make a choice between surrendering their life to the living God and losing their job, or choosing to compromise their faith in order to keep their job and their position. It is very easy to say that I would choose God; but when people actually are faced with making that choice, their actions might be different. The fact is that everyone wants to succeed in life. People, who do not have a biblical view on work, think that working as a businessman, or a nurse, or a teacher is not directly serving God! Some people do not think about living out their faith at work from Monday to Saturday because they don't believe their daily work counts as serving God. For them, they believe that only what they do in church or for the church counts as spiritual engagement. If people are not serving God when they are at their job during the week, who are they serving? If they are not doing their daily work for the Lord, for whom are they working? The Holy Scriptures says "And whatever you do in word or *deed, do everything in the name of the Lord Jesus, giving thanks to God the Father through Him." (Colossians 3:17). There will always be a choice to make. You either choose to do the will of God or not, whether working in your profession or whatever you are doing. You can imagine a question that was resonating in Sandra's audience's mind about the choices her father had to make living in a communist society **(MN)***

Professional success in the Russian economic system is based on loyalty to the communist party rather than on job skills or knowledge. Disciplined obedience along party lines, not training or professional knowledge, is what receives official recognition. These systems become inefficient and corrupt. They discourage innovation or risk taking, and rely on inciting fear and distrust to keep people submissively in line.

Outside the official political party, the average everyday people in a communist society still need a means to sustain themselves and their families. In the halls of government, you may have inefficiency and maneuvering through protocols; but on the ground, the majority of people are just trying to feed their families and keep their jobs. They aren't as loyal to the communist party in their hearts as they portray in their public behavior. They just do what they have to do to feed their families and stay alive. Therefore, whether in low levels within the party or outside the party, the system itself imposes the need for a bartering mechanism among friends or acquaintances where goods bartered are taken from within the system

In the Soviet Union, joining the communist party was assumed and expected when a person achieved a certain level of professional expertise or experience. My father had a deep-rooted personal hatred for the communist system; and he never joined the party. Although my father was quite successful in getting promotions due to his work ethic and commitment, he tried very hard to avoid any opportunity that would lead to an invitation for joining the party. He worked hard inside the system until people would start encouraging him to join the party explaining the perks and benefits of doing so. He would never elaborate why he wouldn't join. He did his best to grow in his positions; but he would not compromise his core values and join the communist party. He would just leave a job gracefully whenever he sensed matters moving in that direction.

It is really remarkable how he was able to do that. I think God's hand was already on my father because he was able to attain a variety of different jobs when he needed them. One time, he got a civilian job on a naval ship. He distinguished himself as an excellent worker, quick learner, and was getting along well with everyone. Even the Captain of the ship noticed his work. Things seemed to be working well and life felt good; until it did not.

One day when they were out to sea, my father was called into the Captain's quarters, without a hint of what the meeting was about. The Captain was sitting behind his desk with a letter in his hand. My father had been doing a good job and was well liked so he wasn't really worried—but he was always a little wary. There was always a tentative, anxious feeling in his stomach that he lived with every day in his present life. It had just become a natural part of him over the years. My father had moved on previously from other jobs so he never assumed a guaranteed longevity at any position.

The captain's eyes looked serious as he silently handed my father the letter to read. As my father read the words, the Captain asked, "Is it true what this letter states?" The letter was exposing my father's family and who he was.

"Yes, Sir." my father quietly mumbled, handing the letter back to the Captain. I cannot imagine the emotions that would have been coursing through his body, not being sure of the Captain's next steps and expecting the worst of the unknown consequences. I cannot imagine the frustration he must have felt at continually having to restart his life and inevitably always needing to move on in order to avoid being caught. A future filled with uncertainty and unknown is hard to endure.

As they sat in silence for what seemed an eternity, the Captain took out his cigarette lighter and burned the letter until it was just a pile of ashes in the ashtray. He looked at the ashtray as he said, "A letter? What letter? No letter arrived here because I know nothing about this situation. I never received it or saw it. Yura, I did hear that you have a family emergency and you have to leave to go home."

Then he said, "You will leave when we dock at the next port, but I will not see you between now and then.

As my father stood up to leave, the Captain continued, "Remember, I never saw a letter. We never talked about this." He paused and extended his hand and said: "Yura, you are a fine young man. Good luck to you. Your father would be proud."

My father nodded, shook his hand and left to gather his things. When the ship returned to port; he left the ship and once more, he was starting over again.

The choice to not join a communist party eventually led to a new beginning in a new foreign land. We can read in the Holy Scriptures how and where the choices of some people led them in their path of life. Those who knew God made their choices so as to please Him in everything they did. They were serving Him within the frame of doing their daily work. The choice of Joseph not to sleep with his master's wife when he was working in the house of Potiphar, an officer of Pharaoh, led him into a prison. The choice of Daniel's friends not to compromise and worship the king of Babylon as they were doing their job led them into a furnace. The list is very long and yet there is good news. Those people who made the choice to honor God and to surrender to his Lordship, despite the suffering and the persecution, were rewarded by God. Not only did the Lord honor their faith and give them a reward that was not perishable, but He demonstrated His power through their lives so that they impacted their generation in remarkable ways. That is why we can read about their stories today in the Holy Scriptures. As people read and see the fingerprint of God in this story, they can also learn to look at their own story and realize how present the same God is in their life *today, even in the darkest times. Can you imagine where the choices of Sandra's father will lead him? **(MN)***

My father did not have time to indulge in self-pity for very long. After 1927 when his family estate was raided and he was released from prison, he survived by continually being on the move with different jobs. He needed to keep restarting life over and over, job after job to avoid having his family identity uncovered. He was especially motivated as he had to find ways to support his mother and the two younger siblings who were still living in abject poverty. They had been forced from their home wearing only their night clothes in the dark of night and thrown into the home of the poorest people on the estate. Now my father became their only means of support because no one would chance giving provisions to anyone labelled as Kulak. It would potentially compromise their own safety to be viewed as accomplices helping people that the Communists deemed as "enemies of the state".

In those years that followed, he would routinely leave money, staples and food supplies in various designated clandestine areas in the woods for his family to later pick up. He couldn't risk going back to the village and drawing attention to his family in the midst of the uncertain social upheaval in the country; but he needed to care for them. It was a means of survival for all of them until the political climates in the Russia settled into a level of safer stability. He was quietly taking care of those he loved even during Stalin's reign of terror.

In 1933, Stalin intentionally created a man-made famine in Ukraine by exporting ALL the wheat that Ukraine produced causing a severe famine throughout the land. On final count, it led to the estimated deaths of 5 to 8 million people. (A detailed, historic account of the Holodomer is written within my mother's story in Part II.) It threw the whole country into a food crisis and starvation. Parents would not let their children out of their sight for fear they would be kidnapped and eaten. My mother told me stories of children she knew who were abducted, never to be seen again. People sometimes mentioned a need to sacrifice children in order to survive.

The famine, called the Holodomor, was especially deadly because, in concert with Stalin's intentional famine, he also ordered that the Kulaks "be eradicated as a class" enhancing the chaos among the farming population even further. All of this was done in order to facilitate Stalin's 5 Year Plan for the collectivization of private farmland. Massive raids and arrests continued during that time and the people lived under an underlying atmosphere of constant fear and oppression.

My father's life had already been shattered into destruction by the horrific night raid on his family home, his father's execution, and denying his heritage in exchange for his life. The Holodomer raised supporting his remaining family to even a higher level of challenge. Food supplies were hard to obtain. He had to find ways to keep his mother and siblings from the brink of starvation. Restarting his professional life each time his family heritage was about to be exposed became a career. My father told my sisters and me that no matter how good the job seemed or how well life appeared to be, he lived every day looking over his shoulder with uneasiness. At work, every time someone with authority knocked on his office door, he caught his breath and a knot grew in his stomach, as he would search the person's face to see if this might be that inevitable time.

Decades
This went on for decades!
I cannot even imagine!!!!

My father's sole goal became to survive sufficiently so that he could support the three other family members who were counting on him. He was living amidst this turmoil without fully understanding eternal life, and God's loving provision for mankind through Jesus Christ. Today, we are blessed to understand God's promises for us. Our experiences, guided by the Holy Spirit, encourage us to trust God through hard times. I am amazed at the strength of the human spirit; and at God's mercy to provide my father with stamina to endure life before my father had any idea personally of God's loving kindness.

As years passed, the political climate in the country stabilized to a more routine but still a restricted existence. By then, the Moscow regime had eradicated all counter opposition and internal struggles diminished as the hierarchy of power became stronger and more defined within the party. People learned how to live and navigate under oppressive conditions.

With time my father's personal character and his willingness to work hard, helped his professional growth significantly. The lumber and forestry had become the second largest industry in the Ukraine and my father found a niche. He worked his way up to being in charge of one of the larger pine forests in Ukraine in the village of Yasnozir'ya, about three hours south of Kyiv, where he met my mother. They married and were beginning to slowly prosper. Even then, he faithfully continued to be available to his other family members. The siblings were grown and they were managing more independently on their own. Providing for their mother was now a shared responsibility among the three children and leaving supplies in the woods was a thing of the past. Meeting each other face to face became a little safer and thus possible. These meetings happened only occasionally, in quiet rural areas, and always with a sense of caution and guard present in the air.

Finally, my father had attained a good style of life in comparison to past years. They worked hard. They had warm clothing and shelter, and plenty of food on the table which they often enjoyed in the company of family and friends. My father was well liked by the people that he worked for. He was even more liked by the people that worked for him in the forest and the people that lived in the village. That was because my father lived out his values of generosity and kindness toward others less fortunate. These values, that he learned from his father as a boy, now had many opportunities to blossom because of the position he held professionally. With the size of the state-owned operation that he was overseeing, he continually had opportunities to siphon off small amounts of surplus and direct them to the personal needs of his workers and others. There was many a village home that was repaired because building supplies clandestinely appeared with no one quite knowing the source of the gift.

My father told a story of an elderly widow whose house was so rundown that it was scheduled to be condemned as uninhabitable and she had no place to go. Of course, there were men living in the village that would gladly do the repair work; but no one could get supplies for the repairs. One day my father was walking down the street, and the widow saw him and came running over to him. She dropped on her knees sobbing and started kissing his feet while thanking him for the building supplies that had unexpectedly shown up in her front yard a week ago. He slowly stooped down and kindly picked her up. He looked gently but firmly into her eyes and said, "Dear Babushka, I do not know what you are talking about. I would love to take credit for that type of kindness and generosity, but it was not me. I don't know you so I am not aware of your troubles. I know nothing about what you are saying, but I am happy for your blessing. You need to thank God for this great gift that He provided and may He continue to bless you many times more.

For me, this story just shows how much children absorb about life from watching their parents. Much of our adult core values and opinions are formed by what we see rather than what we are told. A parent's behavior is a silent communication that speaks loudly and deeply into a child's heart.

The start of WWII had little effect on Ukraine and Russia, until the Germans started to invade Russia. Despite the fact that Stalin had tried to eradicate Ukrainian culture, history, and language, Ukrainian patriotism was strong in the people's hearts and they yearned to be free. They saw an opportunity to escape from under the tyranny and oppression of communism and welcomed the Germans with open arms. They thought the Germans would be their liberators, until the historically harsh Russian winter set in and the Germans were forced to retreat.

Although my father and his whole family were living well above the starvation level that they previously had experienced, my father still had a deep wound in his heart from his time in the prison and denouncing his family name. He had proven himself to be an excellent worker and a kind person. As I previously mentioned, he was well liked. He knew that many people did not agree with the policies of the communist government. The ordinary working people did not have negative reactions against the Kulak class. After the Germans invaded and occupied Ukraine (essentially liberating it), my father decided he would reclaim his family name and hopefully succeed in restoring his father's reputation—and by extension—that of his family.

He went to the officials in authority above him and confessed, "Here's who I really am; and I don't really care what your thoughts are on the subject. My father was generous and kind to the people that worked for him. I have always respected, admired and honored my father. I never denounced my father in my heart. I only signed the papers under duress to get out of jail to save my own life, which he would have wanted me to do. I am cleaning my slate. I am proud of the Didenko name and have no reason to apologize that we were part of the Kulak class."

I am certain it was quite a shock factor to his superiors, but my father took it even a step further and he put an ad in the paper saying the same thing. I imagine that he must have felt a surge of freedom in his heart for the first time in years. The grief and guilt that he had carried around with him was gone and he saw these past years as only a 20-year hiccup on the map of a lifetime journey. Nothing could be worse than what Stalin had already done to Ukraine. My father had to have been so relieved and at peace to bring honor back to his name; and to be able to tell his family, "We can again be publicly proud and hold our heads high about who we are."

Sadly, that feeling of peace and emotional healing did not last long. Instead, it quickly began to feel more like an ironic twist to a bad plot in a Hollywood movie. After publicly proclaiming who he was, reclaiming his family name and denigrating the Russians who had taken over his beloved country by force, he saw the expected outcome of the war turn quickly in the wrong direction. The Germans were unprepared for the severe cold and wet Russian winter and were forced to start retreating. Those he thought would liberate Ukraine were now running from Stalin......And now, my father had a life changing problem again!

Almost everyone hearing or reading this story might be surprised about several things. Mr. Didenko, Sandra's father, was so generous, courageous, and determined to offer the best he could to his family and to the people around him, that he took the risk to claim back part of his real identity -- despite the high price to pay. The surprise is that this did not make his life better. In fact, things became worse as the government of his time was trying to eradicate the Ukrainian people. One question remains: Was God still there at work and what will happen next to Mr. Didenko?

Before moving forward to discover what will happen next in this story, people need to be aware of something! It is possible to have hatred against a nation, a tribe, a language, or a group of people because of the injustice that took place in history. In the Bible, we can read about the climate between the Jewish people and the Samaritans in the Messiah's time. I challenge you to go and read again the story of what happened between the Samaritan woman and Jesus Christ, in John chapter 4 in the Bible. One sentence in John 4:9 says, "The Samaritan woman said to Him, 'How is it that you a Jew, ask for a drink from me, a woman of Samaria?' (For Jews have no dealings with Samaritans)." The Jews hated the Samaritans because of their past history but Jesus did not hate them. In fact, He loved them as He loves all people! Just as the Ukrainians are invited to love the Russians now, despite the cruelty and the offenses of their government leaders, are we not invited to love the nations that caused injustices to our nation? (MN)

Part 2: Leaving and Cleaving

Chapter 1 - A Time of Tough Decisions

Living under the communist regime had a lot of uncertainty just by itself. The war made things even more complicated after the German occupation. It was impossible to function in a normal fashion because people did not know what to expect. They feared returning back to Soviet occupation because they would be suspected of collaboration with the Germans. At the same time, the Germans routinely arrested and indiscriminately executed people that they suspected of being Russian nationalists. No one felt safe as it became harder to discern truth from deception as stories and rumors continued to circulate. Some ranger officials from the forestry operation where my father worked had been arrested and taken from their homes never to be heard from again.

Then, more consistent rumors were circulating that the Germans were retreating at a fast pace. People began to be afraid to sleep in their homes. Men especially started to go into hiding and sometimes would sleep in the forest for many nights at a time. My father was one of those men. The war front was moving closer to the village where my mother and father were living. Sometimes they heard the sounds of fighting in the distance. Whether asleep or awake, their minds and bodies were in a constant state of alert.

My father may not have made the best choice by revealing who he was when he did; and as a result of that choice, he was now forced to make another decision. He could stay and face possible life events far worse than he had previously experienced — probably a tortured execution; or he could take a risk on something even more unknown and try to escape with the retreating German front. He already had one close call where he was stopped on the road coming home, dragged into a barn and interrogated by some German soldiers at gun point. By a miracle from God, they let him go. That incident allowed him to clearly see that actually there was only one choice and that was to leave because nothing could be more dangerous for him than the risk of staying in Ukraine.

Sometimes in our own lives, we make choices that force us into action. My father had been quietly running for many years now. He had managed to change jobs and rise professionally often. However, now he no longer had any place to run. It is similar to the story of Jacob in the Bible. Jacob was always running. He ran from his brother Esau. He ran from his father in law Laban. Jacob did not listen to what God had been saying to him. Then the day came where he decided to go back to where God had created his destiny—his father's house. (Genesis 25-33). In a similar fashion, my father was starting on a journey that his Heavenly Father had planned for him, but he just didn't know the plan or destination yet.

In that moment my father only knew that he had to leave and take his chances heading west as dangers surrounded him from both the Germans and the Soviets. It was late autumn. Winter was coming and my mother was pregnant with me. The timing could hardly be worse. He knew it was going to be a dangerous and physically horrendous trip, so he gave my mother a choice.

After telling her about the incident with the German soldiers, he said, "I have no choice. I have to leave. On the other hand, you have a choice whether to go with me or stay here in the village with your whole family. You have three grown brothers; and they very willingly will assume the responsibility of taking care of you and the baby. You both will be safe and well provided for, as would be expected of them. When I leave, I will most likely die on the road. However, if I stay here I will absolutely be hunted down and executed. "I would rather die trying to find a better life than stay here to be continually worried about running into death around each corner."

Then he said to my mother, "I have to give you a choice. You can come with me or you can stay here safely with your family. I will understand either way. I won't judge. If I get out, I maybe can send for you after the war. It won't be forever, but if you are coming, we have to go soon."

My mother, despite the definite challenges of the road and possible death, chose to follow my father rather than the safety and warm comforts of home and family. I cannot imagine that she could actually visualize how hard the journey would get. She had no idea where this choice was going to take her. I think she actually felt safer beside my father no matter the risk she was taking or the dangers she would be facing. I am grateful for her courage, wisdom, and willingness to sacrifice the security of what she knew for the dangers of the unknown. I also am thankful for her courage to follow my father. I think having my mother and I with him pushed him harder to make it. We may have made the actual traveling more difficult, but we made the journey more meaningful.

At this point of the story, one big question as a leader that still crosses my mind is how can someone know the right choice to make when he is facing a dilemma. This is especially challenging when you have not been raised with experiences of hearing from God! It seems that the decision to take the risk to follow her husband was a step of faith as well as loyalty and faithfulness to her spouse. In that sense, the decision would have come out of love, faithfulness and loyalty to God. **(MN)**

There were so many decisions and so little information. It might be tough for you living in the 21st century to imagine this situation. We can text instantly all around the world, a phone call can be made across all international borders, and we can watch world events as they happen live on television or social media. My parents knew very little about Europe and even less about the United States _ only what they may have read in articles or books. Nothing current. My mother had not traveled outside her village. There were no videos of people living in other places in the world. There were many risk laden unknowns!

The next morning, my parents packed their belongings within a couple hours into a covered wagon, hitched two horses to it, and set out to meet up with a small group of people. The group consisted of two other families and two single men who all had made similar life changing decisions. In a month or so, the challenges of winter would be added to what they were already facing with the challenges of war. They didn't jump in their cars and crank up the heat and set out with a planned itinerary. They were more like a group of pioneers setting out on the road with their faces pointing west; but how far west, for how long and where they would end up, no one knew. They slowly moved along the backroads avoiding the front lines, and trying to navigate as far away from the war activity as possible in order to be safe. They were feeling the faint signs of winter slowly getting closer as sometimes they had to travel in cold mist and rain, trudging on muddy, wet roads with tired hungry horses that needed grass and rest. They asked people living along the way for shelter to rest the night and catch some sleep. If no shelter was available, they slept under trees or under their wagons. They used bushes for bathrooms and hay for beds. Most of the time, they had to camp on the ground outdoors as they traveled. The harsh conditions of winter were coming with no relief in sight. It was a long, cold, icy winter in 1944.

In the last few months, the war situation became clear that the Germans were unable to create a counter offensive and they definitely were in full retreat mode. For my parents and their small entourage, this meant there was no turning back. They had to be intentional to move west with the retreating German front wherever that took them. They continued to stay off the main roads because it was filled with military vehicles. They asked people in villages for help to get to the safer side roads through villages where they could let the horses eat on the side of the road and allow everyone to recover from exhaustion. After a few days of rest, they often were forced to take the central road trying to make more progress. This always was covered in dirt and mud from passing tanks and military vehicles. Motor vehicles and wagons alike were breaking down and getting stuck in the mud. The road was also filled with an endless moving river of refugees pulling carts and wagons through the mud. Deep piles of dirt bordered both sides of the road.

Chapter 2 – Sandra's Birth

As the weather became colder, the muddy roads began to freeze making them better, but the living conditions became proportionately worse in the cold. The group tried to find village people who would let them stay in their homes or barns in exchange for several days work. People would let the women use their kitchens to cook food for the road. Men bought supplies and cared for the horses and made repairs to the wagons. Life was becoming more routine even under duress, as the deep winter snows and icy winds set in. They were moving west slowly with the Germans in front of them and the Russians behind them.

By March 1944, the group had made it through the worst part of winter. Though it was the end of March, the weather continued to be either cold rain, snow or a mixture of both so the women mostly rode in the wagons while the men continued to walk and lead the horses. One particular day, my mother started to feel funny about midmorning. I will let her tell you about that day in her own words.

"About 10 or 11 o'clock in the morning, I suddenly experienced a very strange and unusual pain. I got very frightened; but I thought that maybe I had been sitting funny or maybe just sitting too long. Sometime later, the pain repeated itself. I sat very quietly in the wagon and did not tell anyone. The pain started coming in waves and the intervals between the pains were getting shorter. By 4 o'clock I could stand it no longer but instead of screaming I just clenched my teeth hard to keep them from chattering. I finally called to my husband who was walking in the mud behind the wagon trying to push it because the horses were struggling to pull the wagon. I told him that I thought the baby was coming. There was not much to do. We had only covered 5 km since early morning that day and it was now getting dark. We still did not have a place to stop for the night and there were no villages in sight. Anywhere we looked, we just saw bare fields and artillery. The men conferred with each other and decided to turn left off the road and go across the field, hoping that beyond the hill there would be a village. Once off the road, the wheels got stuck deep in the mud and the horses could not pull the wagon especially since we were going uphill. The men pushed each wagon helping the horses to reach the top. It took several hours and it was now dark but we did see some lights in the distance. The horses were tired. We had to stop frequently to let them rest.

Everybody was exhausted by the time we reached the lights of the village. I was sitting in the wagon, wet and shaking from the cold rain with my teeth chattering uncontrollably. There was a sentry at the main entrance to the village. The German guard stopped us at the gate asking us who we were and where did we come from. Usually the Germans were not kind as they were retreating; but this time the sentry was very understanding and helpful. He took us to the nearest farm house and then further back to what looked like a barn. He began shouting to the soldiers sleeping on the floor to wake up. These poor soldiers were also fatigued from a hard day on the road. They must have gotten warm lying in the hay; and now they were ordered to get up and go out into the cold. They started gathering their things and walking out grumbling and quite unhappy. There was a stove at one end of the room away from the hay piles on the other side. I went and stood close to the stove enjoying its warmth. I could barely tolerate the fits of pain; and my teeth were chattering so loud that everyone could hear them. I tried to clench my jaws tight with my hands, but that did not help at all. The other women started to make beds in the hay. One woman pushed some hay closer to the warm wall, covering it with an old cloth to make a bed for me; but I was more comfortable sitting on an old bench against the wall. She told me to lie down. In the meanwhile, the men were outside un-harnessing and feeding the horses and giving them water.

Sometime later everyone came into the barn, and settled down on the hay beds. My husband sat down by the bench and was waiting to see what would happen next. Finally, the pains became so strong that I asked one of the women how much longer were the pains going to continue. She told me I would be screaming so loudly that everyone would wake up and leave the room. I got up to go to the bathroom; but suddenly I felt like something was preventing me from walking. The woman told me to lay down quickly. I turned back to the bench; and just put my knee on it to lie down, when another wave of labor pain hit me, and the baby fell out into the hay...a little girl who cried right away. The woman jumped up and ran toward me. She finished the birthing procedure with my husband helping...both doing it for the first time. However, we had nothing to wrap the baby in. I had prepared some things for the baby but they were packed in our bags in the wagon outside. One of the single men had a clean undershirt that he had brought in with him for a change of clothes. He gave it to us to wrap the baby in. I was relieved because we were fighting a flea infestation.

They put me on my back in the hay covered with an old cloth and gave me the baby. She cried for a little while and then got quiet. Everyone quieted down and finally went back to sleep. In the morning, the men decided to stay on an extra day because of me; and everyone welcomed an extra day of rest after the hard journey the previous day. The women decided to bake some bread for the journey. The plans were to make a full tub of dough and let it rise over night. Then bake the bread in the morning. Eat some for breakfast and pack the rest to take with us. Everything went according to plan and we went to bed. However, at three in the morning the German sentry came running in shouting for us to leave as the Russians were only 3 km away. We jumped up, in whatever we were wearing. The women quickly grabbed whatever we had with us while the men were harnessing the horses. I shot up as if nothing had happened to me. Overcome with fear, I could not feel the after pain of giving birth. My husband brought a blanket and pillow from the wagon that I had saved for our baby; and gathered the rest of our things. I stretched out the blanket and put the pillow and baby inside. I tied the blanket corners together as if it were an envelope using the open corner to cover the baby's head so she could have some air but still stay warm.

My husband loaded up our bags on top of the cart and I climbed next to them on my knees holding the baby. There was not a lot of space left. We decided to leave the village using back roads that lead away from the direct fighting but did eventually require crossing a river." *

* The above section is translated from a personal memoir written by my mother when she was in her eighties. She lived to be 98 years old.

It is hard to imagine the circumstances of my birth. No recording of birth certificates or pictures. No parties. No balloons. No warmers or soft jammies. I didn't even have diapers. It is even harder to imagine the circumstances in which I survived the first 2 years of life. However, it is impossible to believe that I NEVER in my 80 years of life have been seriously ill enough to need hospitalization except for the births of my two children. Now as a mother myself, I still cannot even imagine how my mother endured it all.

Remember, my parents had been living well in Ukraine when the Germans marched into the country during WWII. They had warm homes, plenty of food, a working well for fresh water, and many comforts to enjoy. The nation was at war, but the military front was far away and they lived in relative comfort. Now they were cold, wet, and back on muddy roads, struggling with weak horses who clumsily were pulling cumbersome wagons, occasionally dodging missiles and frequently being trapped in gun crossfire. I had my mother with me when my children were born in the warmth and safety of a clean aseptic hospital. My mother had no relatives around when I was born, and no way to even tell her family the good news. Her living relatives who remained in Ukraine didn't even know if my mother was still alive until 16 years after my birth, when we received our first written communication from behind the Iron Curtain through the Red Cross at an Easter Sunday church service in 1960.

Even under these difficulties, they found joy and blessing in the midst of the challenges. There was a woman in the group who had already given birth to two children so she could explain to my mother what would happen and how to care for the baby. I was born in Ukraine, something my father was very proud of and my mother joked that it was intentional. She would laugh when telling the story and say that my father traveled slower so I would be born while still in Ukraine.

This part of the story is a good reminder that every birth is a miracle from God! He is the Creator and only He creates life. Every birth is special and every baby is precious and unique. A birth circumstance might be difficult and challenging, but God is always at work. Who else can save a baby's life in a situation like Sandra's birth if it is not the Lord? He preserved Moses' life in the book of Exodus in a basket floating in a river. Jesus the son of God was born in a manger where the farm animals lived. The point here is that no matter the circumstances, God, the life giver, is always at work when a baby is to be born. (Psalm139:13-16, Isaiah 44:24, Colossians 1:15-17).

God's heart is looking for many Sandras to be born no matter their circumstances. God has a plan for every baby including those born into tough conditions like Sandra's or the ones who are abandoned on the street. God is always happy for people like Sandra's mother who decided to have their baby despite their poverty and their challenging conditions.. As you keep reading the story you will discover that God has a wonderful plan for people like Sandra as well! **(MN)**

Chapter 3 – A Hard Life Before the Journey

My mother Dasha was destined to a hard life both physically and emotionally from childhood but was blessed abundantly in her later years after all her previous years of hardship. She was born into a family of 3 brothers which quickly toughened her during her early childhood years. My mother's family was sufficiently well provided for. You can imagine as the only daughter, she was the "little princess" in her father's eyes and was very close to him. She was 12 years old when she encountered a monumental emotional trauma caused by Stalin's famine that the Ukrainian people had to endure in 1932-1933.

The Soviet government was still in its infancy and trying to build a stronghold over Ukraine. These were unsettling times with a lot of angst and fear injected into communities with rumors of arrests and unexplainable disappearances. To spotlight its severity, Ukrainians call the famine Holodomor, a term derived from the Ukrainian words for hunger (*holod*) and extermination (*mor*).

Holodomor was a man-created **famine** that convulsed **Ukraine as** a Soviet Republic in 1932 and peaking in the spring of 1933. Its severity was increased by a series of political decisions made in Moscow that were aimed only at the Ukraine and its extinction as a people group and a culture.

The famine was started when Joseph Stalin, head of the newly formed Soviet Union, decided to collectivize Ukrainian agriculture in 1929. The government organized groups of the Soviet Communist army (Bolsheviks) who systematically attacked and forced peasant landowners to relinquish their land, personal property, and housing in order to allow the government to then turn all private lands into government owned collective farms. They either deported or executed the so-called kulaks—wealthier peasants—as well as any peasants who resisted collectivization. This led to an extreme drop in wheat production, a disruption of the rural economy, and huge food shortages. It also sparked a series of peasant rebellions, including armed uprisings, in parts of Ukraine.

The rebellions worried Stalin. He was concerned by the anger and resistance to the agricultural collectivization policy within the Ukrainian Communist Party, and feared a wide spread national revolution. The leadership of the Soviet Communist Party, made a series of decisions to widen and deepen the famine in the Ukrainian countryside. Farms, villages, and whole towns in Ukraine were placed on blacklists and prevented from receiving food. Peasants were forbidden to leave the Ukrainian Republic in search of food. Despite growing starvation, government food requisitions were increased and humanitarian aid was not allowed to be provided. The crisis peaked in the winter of 1933, when organized groups of communist police ransacked the homes of peasants and took everything edible, from crops to personal food supplies to pets, who could be considered a source of food in desperation. Sometimes, the KGB would stop young mothers with baby carriages to check if the infant's bottle was filled with milk (or sometimes grain as a means of hiding seeds for future planting. In either case, whatever the bottle was filled with, the KGB would pour it out and trample it into the ground.

These atrocities against humanity was reinforced by hateful rhetoric emanating from the Kremlin focused on extermination of the Ukrainian people and culture. By 1934 some 5.7-8.7 million Ukrainians perished of hunger. Instances of cannibalism as well as lawlessness, theft, and lynching spread throughout the countryside.

The famine was accompanied by a parallel track, a broad assault on Ukrainian identity. While peasants were dying by the millions, the Soviet secret police were targeting the Ukrainian political establishment and cultural intelligentsia. The famine provided cover for a campaign of repression and persecution that was carried out against the Ukrainian cultural and religious leaders. Ukrainization, which encouraged the Ukrainian language and culture was abruptly halted. Moreover, anyone still connected to the short-lived Ukrainian People's Republic was intentionally targeted and either jailed, sent to forced-labor camps or executed. (Ukrainian People's Republic was an independent government that had been established in June 1917 during the February Revolution.

It was immediately dismantled by the Bolsheviks after they conquered all of the Ukrainian territory.)

The news of the famine was deliberately silenced by Soviet Party officials to the international community. Western journalists based in Moscow were instructed not to write about it. Stalin went so far as to repress the results of a national census taken in 1937. (The administrators of that census were arrested and murdered, in part because the figures revealed the decimation of Ukraine's population.)

Although the famine was discussed during the Nazi occupation of Ukraine in WWII, it again became taboo to discuss during the postwar years. The first public mention of it in the Soviet Union was in 1986 after the Chernobyl Nuclear Power Plant disaster. (That disaster too was initially kept secret by the Soviet authorities.)

The deadly famine inflicted on Ukraine was officially denied by the Kremlin for over a half a century. This tragic event continues to play a large role in the public memory of the Ukrainian people, especially following their independence after the Soviet Union dissolved in 1991. Since then, many monuments commemorating the Holodomor have been erected; and Holodomor Remembrance Day is nationally observed on the fourth Saturday of November every year.

While reading again about the famine there is a poignant need to point out a fact. Disasters like famines, war, economic crises, or genocides don't come from the

Creator of the universe. They are the consequences of mankind turning away from God's will and pursuing a path not aligned with God's values. Unfortunately, some people including leaders, often make the choice to pursue sensual satisfaction, material possessions, and self-centered importance. That is how evil, horrific concepts like the Holodomor get created causing devastation to vast portions of humanity.

Again, considering how severe and wicked the famine was, there is a question that people ask most often: "Where was God?" People usually ask that question out of their naiveness of who God is, not out of compassion and maturity. Presently, there are many man-made famines in the world. People looked at the genocide that took place in Rwanda in 1994 and they asked the same question: "Where was God?" It is good to ask those questions to God, especially when it is painful. Therefore, does this question help people turn back to God or alternatively, prove that God is bad? Do political leaders lead people into a mess because God doesn't want to lead them? No, it is because they refuse to listen ("Shema") to God?

This morning I was reflecting with my children about listening to God, about the word Shema that I studied during my Master in Leadership with Youth with A Mission. The word Shema means "to listen and to obey" in Hebrew. My children said it means to do what God asks you to do! The Lord in his nature and his character is good, just, merciful, and no evil comes out from Him. When mankind chooses to listen, to fear God, and to obey Him, it is expressed in human society by *justice, mercy, generosity, and safety. When people choose to turn away, they sow destruction and wickedness in their society.*

God's heart is consistently broken when people and leaders choose to reject Him. It is because of God's rescue and intervention in the midst of mankind's bad choices that famines and disasters can even be relieved. Jesus ("Yaweh") is always there to save and help. God is always calling everyone, including leaders, to turn away from their evil ways and to come back to Him to live! Therefore, people can decide to focus on the tragedy, or people can choose to express their emotions and seek help from the loving God who is always there to rescue, to comfort, and to restore. The Almighty God is the only One who can give life to the dry bones! (Ezekiel 37:4,14). (MN)

One night during this terrible time of fear and famine, the rumors of arrests became a personal reality to my mother when the KGB came in the dark to their door and took her father away for questioning. She never saw him again. Her mother tried multiple times to desperately find out what happened to him and what the charges were for his arrest. She went to the authorities so many times that she was finally told not to come back or there would be further repercussions against her children and her. Life was never the same again for my mother both emotionally and physically. The emotional trauma of losing her father - a deep love attachment suddenly and irreparably severed - at the formative age of twelve years old was something she could never completely get over. That severe loss affected her for the rest of her long life.

The family never recovered. Their existence fell to such a poverty level that her mother would boil unwashed potatoes for their dinner so that the dirt on the potato would help fill their stomachs. My mother would beg my grandmother to wash her potato because she would rather be less full but taste the real potato.

Several years after my mother's father disappeared, the collectivization of farms was completed. Families were assigned an allotment of rows to care for in the collectivized fields. The number of rows in the allotment was dependent on the number of family members in the household. There was only one younger brother left at home (too little to work) and my grandmother who was trying to scrape out a living by working and bartering in the black markets. So the three person allotment assigned to their family, all fell on my mother's young teenage shoulders. She had to walk five miles just to get to the assigned field. She would get up in the early morning hours, and start walking while it was still dark so she could get to the field to start working at dawn as it became light. She told my sisters and me that one time she had gotten to the field when the sun was just rising on the horizon. She was so hungry and weak that she sank to her knees and begged God to please fill her stomach so she could feel the sensation of being full just one more time before she died. She always ended that story, saying that God had answered her prayer so abundantly by bringing her to America that for the rest of her life, she could never throw food away, and out of respect for that we, the three sisters, still either finish everything on our plates or save the food for later.

Let's go on with the Story!

Relieved that the birth of a baby was successfully behind them, the little wagon train of families continued on. They followed back roads along a river, camping along the way, always trying to avoid the military and any battle activity.   It was weeks before they managed to find a reasonable crossing place in the river. It had been raining a lot so the water level on particularly high. This concerned my parents because they only had the weak horses that the Germans left them when they confiscated my parents' original strong ones. During the crossing, my mother said that all you could see above the water level was the horses' ears and mouths gasping for air. Somehow these small horses were able to pull the wagon almost across to the other shore even though many of their belongings had gotten wet because the back half of the wagon ended up under water in the crossing. The strong river current was causing all the wagons to be unstable and pushing the whole wagon train downstream far from the actual road they were aiming to reach. However, as they neared the shore line, they spotted some stumps in the water indicating a gradual incline toward the river bank which then became a symbol of safety and firm ground.

As they tried to navigate the approach up toward the river's edge, one of the wheels on our wagon got caught on something underwater and suddenly flipped the wagon over. My mother had been walking behind the wagon to lighten the load for the horses who were struggling to pull it up the incline. I was laying in the wagon sleeping on top of the baggage. My mother began screaming that the baby was missing. All the men quickly ran to lift the wagon up, knowing the baby was probably trapped under the water. However, when they lifted the wagon upright, there was no baby to be found. It was dusk by now and hard to see. My mom screamed, "I don't have the baby. I don't have the baby!" Everyone stopped and ran to help. Some people looked among the things that were still in the wagon. Others were running in the water along the shore line desperately searching while they picked up the packages that were floating downstream away from the wagon. It was really strange because they could not find the baby dead or alive. And then a woman thought that she saw a package caught in some branches of a bush in the water just about two feet from the shore. She grabbed the bundle and she declared, "Here she is!" I must have gently rolled out and floated face up. I was still sleeping not making a sound which is why they could not find me. I had literally just floated to the point where I got caught in the branches of this bush by the shore. This story is hard for even me to believe! Truly a miracle... one of the many in my life.

(Some people are born requiring more of God's time and attention as an infant than the average person requires their whole life. When my husband wants to pick up the tempo of a dinner conversation with people who do not know us well, he will often say, "What do you think my wife has in common with Moses and Jesus.} It is interesting that when God was creating me, He already knew that all my life, I would require just a little more of

His attention than the average person does. He is faithful and continues to do it right into my silver years. I think He puts in His calendar to remember to check up on me on a regular basis.

There is no doubt that the miracle-working God, was at work! There was poverty, hunger, dangers in an unsafe trip and perils of war; but the Almighty God was watching over these refugee families. Jesus himself was once a refugee in Africa. He understood what was going on with Sandra's family and many others people around her and He did not forsake them. What an amazing God He is! Those who are humble even if they do not believe in Jesus Christ, they can notice that God is there at least to rescue them from a danger or a difficult situation. God is inviting people to humble themselves before Him and to enjoy the loveliest relationship He is offering to mankind! **(MN)**

Chapter 4 - The Long Journey Across Europe

The little wagon train continued its journey across Eastern Europe. There was no designated itinerary with scheduled arrival destinations. They just followed the war front as it moved, exchanged information with other traveling refugees and adjusted plans depending on what was happening with the military maneuvers at the moment. The common goal was to stay as far in front of the Russians' line as possible; and not get caught in a cross fire of bullets or an aerial bombing attack. They travelled on for months staying in people's barns, camping in meadows or near the forest's edge depending on where there was access to water, wood for a fire, and grass for the horses.

It was a challenge to have a newborn. My mother was a petite woman of small build. The stress of the journey and their limited diet of dry bread with pieces of salted pork supplemented with hot watery soup for dinner, left most of the adults malnourished. It was no surprise that the baby had trouble nursing. German soldiers would hear a baby crying and give my mother chocolate. She would chew it up into pieces, put it in a cheese cloth and let me suck on it. My mother had an aluminum cup that she would take with her when she went to knock on a farm house door asking for milk for her baby. Sometimes she would go to 2-3 houses to gather enough milk for a day. She said no matter how austere the living conditions were for the people, no one ever denied her a cup of milk. She would dip a piece of dried bread into the milk and let me suck on it. If there was a shortage of bread, she would dip a piece of cheese cloth into the milk and let me suck that. Eventually I graduated to sipping milk from a spoon so life got a little easier for her.

My diapers were nothing more than torn up rags. She would take my diaper off of me and rinse it out in a puddle and hang it on the wagon hoping it would dry before it was needed again. Often if the weather was bad, she would ring it out and put it against her body in hopes it would dry in time. She always rode in the wagon with her legs folded under her holding me because there was not enough room in the wagon to stretch out her legs. Over time, the familiar repetition of daily activity fell into a routine that provided an eerie peace, even though each day brought its own unexpected surprises along the road. The group had become accustomed to hearing repetitive shots and loud bomb explosions at a distance. These sights and sounds quietly slipped into being part of the routine category. They were grateful and content when the sounds were distant enough that they were not at risk of being hit.

However, frequently they would suddenly become the targets of bullets and bombs. At those times, people would just scatter…anywhere they could hide to feel safe from the shrapnel and the bullets. My mother was with a newborn so it was almost impossible to scurry away in the snow to a hiding place. Often by the time, she was able to pull me out from sleeping amidst the packages and luggage, she would find herself either alone in the middle of a field or sometimes the bombing or shooting from the machine guns would have stopped.

At some point, my mother made the decision to never run but just trust God. When she told me the stories, she said that she just held me really, really tight and prayed that God would either spare both of us or take both of us. She did not want either one of us left behind. She did not want to lose a baby; and she did not want me to survive without her because human life was not valued very highly and I would probably perish by a suffering death anyway. After that decision, for two years shrapnel and bullets would fly by her head while she sat huddled in place. My mother never ran and she never even got a scratch wound.

One afternoon, my parents' little caravan had just set up camp and settled in. My mother was standing in the open holding me, trying to decide where she could bathe me, when suddenly she felt surrounded by a shower of shrapnel from exploding bombs. She dropped to the ground protecting me with her body, as everyone around her ran for cover. When the shower of shrapnel ceased, she stood up only to see the bull that had been grazing about a city block away from her, now lying dead.

Yes, God faithfully honored all of Sandra's mother's continual prayers for protection. It is interesting that both her parents believed in God and had faith to pray even though they did not yet understand the clear gospel message. In Ecclesiastes 3:11, Scripture says that God has put eternity in all our hearts, which prepares any who will sense it, that there is a God and that He cares. Psalm 12:7 records that "He protects those who are oppressed." We clearly see the oppression experienced by both parents. That oppression causes people to pray; and answered prayers help people be comforted that there is a higher being in charge. The Bible says that God is known and makes Himself known. God uses these situations to draw us to Himself. Often, we know He is there, even before we accurately can identify Him. God makes Himself known, not only by placing eternity in our hearts and giving us experiences of answered prayer; but also by observing His creation. In Romans 1:20 the apostle Paul says that "we are without excuse." If you haven't already, we pray that readers like you will sense the presence of God in Sandra's parents' lives and, by extension, you begin to see God active in your life. (RCV)

As they traveled on, our caravan joined up with another group of refugees who were camping in a farmer's field. There was a lot of discussion happening about the best way to cross into Poland. These refugees shared that there was a bridge at the Desna River where the Germans were planning a massive river crossing for their military troops before they blew up the bridge in order to stall the Russian advance. The German commanders were allowing civilians to cross the bridge when the military was not using it for crossing. A multitude of refugees were gathering in that area hoping for an opportunity to cross. Our little caravan decided that it was worth trying to get to the Desna River bridge which was a three to four days journey.

The following day they were back on the road with no time to spare because the Russian soldiers were closing in. My parents were quickly moving forward, trying to reach the bridge to cross over before the Germans finished their military crossing and blew up the bridge. Little did my parents know that while they were trying to get there, the American pilots were already there bombing the bridge at the peak of the military crossing operation and not discriminating between military or civilian targets. When my parents' wagon train arrived, it was frightening to see the aftermath of the destruction.

Those people, who were crossing on the bridge at the time, went down with it. Those waiting to cross on the nearby water edge immediately became a sea of corpses. The carts and trucks lay overturned in the field as far as the eye could see. All the belongings of the refugees were strewn among the vehicles. Fortunately, they had already removed the casualties off the land. The few people that survived said that during the attack, it truly felt like Judgement Day. Refugees, still arriving to the place like my parents, were anxious to quickly leave the area when they saw the horror caused by the bridge destruction. The horrors of the war and the uncertainty of their own lives was too hard to bear visually, so like the others, my parents quickly continued on.

They traveled for two more days along the river bank asking people and trying to locate another bridge. When they finally found another bridge, the German military was crossing there also; but it was a much smaller military operation. With a little bartering and a lot of kindness from the German commanders, they were able to cross into Poland with the German soldiers.

The travels of the little caravan were often filled with unexpected surprises. Once when they entered a town looking for a place to spend the night, the townspeople directed them to an abandoned Polish catholic monastery on the outskirts of town. It was scantly furnished; but as a protection from the weather conditions, it felt like a five-star hotel to them. They spent the next day regrouping. The women tended to the children, prepared food for the road and washed clothes. The men tended to the horses, repaired the wagons, and reorganized for the road. That evening they barely settled down for some well-deserved rest when they heard the sounds of inbound planes and the roar of their engines was getting closer. Everyone rushed out of the building except my mother who was frozen in place by the table where she was changing my diaper. She was in shock trying to figure out what to do when she felt someone pull on her dress. She looked down to find one of the two little Rymski girls, who belonged to one of the families in the caravan, peeking out from under the table. Their parents -- crazy with fear -- forgot them at the house. The little girls were very young but they already knew that one needed to hide...at least under a table.

In days like those, many families became split up and many children were lost never to be found. When the shelling or bombing would start, people immediately scattered trying to find safety. In the bedlam of fear and running for safety, many families – both parents and children -- would easily get separated. Afterwards when they regathered together if someone was missing, it sometimes was impossible to find them no matter how much effort was made. It was a continual heartbreaking situation that could rear its ugly head unexpectedly and all too often.

Fortunately, this episode with the two little girls under the table ended well. The bombs fell but missed them. Following the attack, everyone regathered and regrouped. The people in the caravan were now wide awake and did not feel secure enough to stay in the monastery. They packed up everything and fled into the night.

Listening to this part of Sandra's story, it is evident that God's arms were there to protect them all the time. He is the one who protected Joseph from his brothers and Pharaoh in the Bible. He protected Moses and the nation of Israel from Pharaoh so that we can read their story and know Him more. God protected Rahab and David so that through their offspring He could send the Messiah to save mankind from sin. He protected Sandra so that we can read this story and learn how much He is omnipresent in every generation and always willing to reveal Himself to whoever longs to find Him. You are still alive today for a divine purpose! Despite the mess of this world, God still has a story to write with people who will choose to listen and follow Him. God has a story to write with all people no matter how poor or how weak and vulnerable they are. (MN)

They had been traveling continually since October 1943, surviving the harsh winter and the birth of a baby in early spring. With thankful hearts, they had welcomed the summer months that gave them a little easier life style as they traveled camping outdoors. However, now the autumn chill was one of the first signs of the more severe weather to come as they continued through Poland. They were hoping to reach another country before winter set in... but where to go next???? It was either Romania, Hungary or Czechoslovakia. There were rumors circulating that in Romania everything was taken away from the newly emigrated people; and the people were then sent back to the Soviet Union. These rumors were confirmed by the few people that managed to escape back to Poland. Hungary was presently not officially receiving immigrants; but those, who managed to sneak over the Hungarian border, were allowed to pass through into another country. As for Czechoslovakia, it was deemed unsafe. There were rumors that the Soviets had infiltrated part of that country by parachuting massive numbers of Soviet Partisans by night; and they had a reputatiom for being a very strong, active force to confront.

Soviet Partisans were an underground resistance army/movement trained in guerilla warfare and created by the Russians to disrupt German military networks and economic activity. Because of the inhumane German policies toward civilians, there were similar strong networks engaged in guerilla warfare in almost every German occupied country. By engaging German soldiers in fighting, they were able to preoccupy many German divisions that were sorely needed at the actual battlefront.

My parents feared the Soviet Partisans as much as they feared the Russian army. My father always suspected that the soldiers, who had stopped and dragged him into a barn for interrogation when he and my mother were still living in the village in Ukraine, were Soviet Partisans posing as German soldiers. While traveling, they had encountered a group of them demanding food and clothing. Thankfully, after the supplies were provided, the guerilla fighters moved on. There were rumors that the Soviet Partisans were getting more aggressive. They routinely robbed any travelling refugees that they encountered. Sometimes, they interrogated the refugees trying to get them to join the movement, and killed them if they refused.

The small wagon train finally reached the border of Hungary. There the group evaluated the situation first hand, those with children decided that it was too dangerous to try to sneak across the border to Hungary. The crossing was always carried out clandestinely in the middle of the night. People traveled lightly, leaving their horses and carts behind and crossing with only the belongings that they could carry. All this would be a daunting challenge with small children. The men could not see how they would carry the children as well as sufficient belongings without a wagon. There was also no guaranteed way of keeping the children quiet. An unexpected cry from a baby while they were crossing the border would have been a sure reason for the border patrol to open fire. Those without children found crossing into Hungary by night less daunting and more appealing as a direct route. It soon became clear that it was best for the little caravan to split and go separate ways.

In the end, the Rymsky family with the two little girls and my parents with the baby decided against crossing into Hungary and remained a couple more days as they investigated and created an alternative route. The decision was made! They had no other choice but to press on to Czechoslovakia, hoping for God's mercy.

Whatever would be – would be in God's hands.

How can some people still be alive as they face continual dangers day and night like this? It almost looks like a movie where the key characters will never die. The difference here is that God is the focus and He is the one doing miracles to keep some refugees alive. So, let's keep holding on to the story, and let's be amazed by God's protection on this little traveling party of two families just as He did with Daniel's friends in the furnace (Daniel 3:19-30). **(MN)**

The plan was to move on toward the small part of Czechoslovakia that was still safe and not yet infiltrated with the Soviet partisans. The larger plan was to continue moving quickly and directly to either Germany or Austria depending what they found out from travelers along the road. They traveled through the forest the entire day with fear in their hearts. With God's provision of safety, nothing bad happened. They arrived safely in a large market square filled with travelers, carts and wagons, and horses. My parents were feeling calmer now that they were not as vulnerable; and they welcomed the opportunity to get lost in the mass of gathered people. It felt safer not be singled out by appearance as lonely travelers. They decided to spend the night. The women prepared camp as the men tended to the horses and then circulated among the carts and wagon seeking the latest information from the other travelers.

It was a warm moonlit night that was rare for late autumn. My mother settled me into a makeshift crib hanging under the wagon that my father had made out of sticks and a blanket. Rocking me while lying beside the crib, my mother suddenly heard shots being fired but could not tell if they were fired into the air or at the wagons. No one knew for certain so everyone ran for cover. As usual, my mother stayed and draped her body over the crib, trying to wait out the shots. When the shots finally stopped, she heard people talking but they were voices of strangers. Not far from her were two strange men on a wagon ravaging through all the belongings. One had pulled out a large trunk and was trying to shoot the lock open. When they noticed my mother, they asked her for men's clothing and food. They did not take any of the belongings but they did take a sack of salted bacon and some sugar. They were loading up a horse with their bounty when some rifle shots were again fired (probably a signal to leave) so they quickly finished and rode away. In the morning, they found out that these men were Soviet Partisans rebuilding their supplies at the price of traveling refugees. Everyone was thankful that the price was merely food not a human life.

The following day, they crossed the border into Czechoslovakia and stopped at an abandoned house on the edge of a village. The mayor of the village gave them permission to stay there because he did not like communists and was willing to help refugees traveling through any way that he could. As it began to get dark each night, the adults were terrified of the Partisans coming again. The men would go into the woods to sleep. The women stayed back with the children making beds out of planks of wood covered with hay. They remained there for a week preparing for future travel during the day and repeating the same sleeping ritual during the night. Finally, the little caravan of two families decided to keep moving through Czechoslovakia toward the city of Ostrava.

In a late fall afternoon as they arrived to Bilovec, on the outskirts of Ostrava, and encountered what looked like a permanent setback and possibly the end of not only their quest for freedom but the end of their actual lives. The Russians had infiltrated into that town and were herding all traveling refugees to the train station and loading them onto box cars. The two families got caught up in the herding and were forced onto the boxcars. For three days, they sat in the boxcars waiting for the steam engine to come to pull the train of boxcars back to the motherland, but the engine never came. The Russians finally moved all the captured people to a temporary camp, which was comprised of wooden barracks built around a square of common ground surrounded by a barbed wire fence, to wait until the steam engine arrived. The only redeeming thing was that the Russians turned the operations of the camp over to Slovak authorities who were now in charge of overseeing all its operations; and they were much kinder than the Russians had been.

The only way out of the camp was past a guard house and the refugees were not allowed to leave the camp unless they had a reason and permission from the guard to leave. Rymski and my father thought if they somehow could leave and get back to the Czechoslovakian village on the border where the mayor had been so kind, he might let the two families hide out there again until the immediate dangers of deportation in the boxcars would be resolved. My father told Rymski that he had seen a hole cut in the barbed wire fence when he was surveying the campgrounds. The Slovak police mostly maintained order in the camp but did not pay much attention to the internal happenings in the camp. That night Rymski and my father disappeared and were gone for two days. In the meantime, Rimsky's wife and my mother continued to maintain a normal daily routine. The day after the men disappeared, there was an announcement on a loud speaker bullhorn for all adults to gather in the square for a meeting. My mother stood in the back on the outer edge of the crowd because she had left me asleep and wanted to be able to run back quickly to check on me. A Soviet officer was addressing the crowd, calling for all able-bodied people to join the Soviet Partisans to fight the Germans. One of the Soviet commanders approached my mother to join the nurses' core of the Partisan cause. She told him she had a small baby that she needed to look after. He further interrogated my mother and asked where was her husband to which she replied, "Around here somewhere, but not sure exactly." The Slovak police officer with him said that her husband was most certainly around because orders had come down just that morning saying that no one was allowed to leave the camp without written permission. My mother must have looked frightened or anxious because the Soviet officer turned to her gruffly and told her to go take care of her baby.

The following day was Sunday and the husbands returned to camp as though they had been there all along. They instructed the women to start packing because they were all leaving the camp shortly. The women packed half-heartedly thinking that they would be back in an hour unpacking since no one was being allowed out of the gate. Even though there was not a lot of belongings to pack, the exercise seemed a futile, unnecessary effort to the women.

They loaded up the wagons and proceeded to the gate with an increasing number of curious people gathering and following them to see what was going to happen. When the wagon train stopped at the gate, the Czech guard informed them that he could not let them leave the camp without written permission issued by the commandant's office. The men left the wagons at the gate and asked the guard to wait while they went to the office to get the appropriate documents. The two men walked away toward the office building and stood behind it out of sight of the guard house for a little while. They returned and told the guard that the officer on duty said he was unable to issue any documents to them today because it was Sunday. However, since they were already packed to leave, they should instruct the guard that the commandant gave them verbal permission to leave the camp. Miraculously, the guard simply opened the gate and the wagons drove through, while the group of curious people stood and watched in astonishment of what just happened in front of their eyes.

A miracle very similar to this is recorded in the book of Acts. It is the biblical account of an angel breaking Peter's chains and leading him out of jail. Read the Scriptural account below and you will be able to picture an angel leading Sandra's father and Rymski and their families out of the refugee camp.

In Acts 12:1-11 this is recorded:
About that time Herod the king laid violent hands on some who belonged to the church. He killed James the brother of John with the sword, and when he saw that it pleased the Jews, he proceeded to arrest Peter also. This was during the Feast of Unleavened Bread (Passover). And when they had seized Peter, they put him in prison, delivering him over to four squads of soldiers to guard him, intending after the Passover to bring him out to the people. So Peter was kept in prison, but earnest prayer for him was made to God by the church.

Now when Herod was about to bring him out, on that very night, Peter was sleeping between two soldiers, bound with two chains, and sentries before the door were guarding the prison. And behold, an angel of the Lord stood next to him, and a light shone in the cell. He struck Peter on the side and woke him, saying, "Get up quickly." And the chains fell off his hands. And the angel said to him, "Dress yourself and put on your sandals." And Peter did so. And the angel said to him, "Wrap your cloak around you and follow me." And he went out and Peter followed him. He did not know that what was being done by the angel was real, but thought he was seeing a vision. When they had passed the first and the second guard, they came to the iron gate leading into the city. It opened for them of its own accord, and they went out and went along one street, and immediately the angel left him. When Peter came to himself, he said, "Now I am sure that the Lord has sent his angel and rescued me from the hand of Herod and from all that the Jewish people were expecting." (RCV)

Once past the guard house, the men whipped the horses into a full gallop as they ran toward the nearest forest. They were fearful that the guards would follow them. Once deep in the forest, they hid quietly until night fall; and then proceeded on a couple days' journey back to the village near the border of Czechoslovakia to the kind mayor and the abandoned house where the group had stayed a few weeks earlier. The mayor welcomed them back warmly and they quickly settled into their previous routine - the women and children staying in the house while the men hid outside in the woods to sleep every night. They remained in the village for weeks while the fighting continued until the German troops finally pushed back the Russian army that surrounded the area.

God saved His followers from certain death in prison in a miraculous way. In much the same way, God saved Sandra, her parents and their friends from certain death. He opened the path for this precious wagon train and closed the minds of the guards to provide a safe passage out of the camp. God has performed many miracles in the past and continues to perform them today. We know God is <u>able</u> to do so; yet we do not get to choose when and how He intervenes miraculously. However, should we each look at our own past, we can often see God's hand of protection intervening to change our circumstances or allowing us to escape from dangerous situations. (MN)

Everyone was very anxious to start traveling on the road again. As soon as it felt safe enough, they began to travel to Banska Bystritsa near Bratislava in Czechoslovakia. A third family that they met in the village asked if they could join the little entourage on the journey. It was a husband and wife along with her father and her uncle. The woman was fluent in German. They had ended up in a camp similar to that of my parents; but with her proficiency in German, she was able to convince the Slovak commander that she was German which allowed her family to leave the camp.

The little entourage spent the coldest part of the winter in Banska Bystritsa. The men found work using their horses to deliver wood and other materials from the forest to various people in the village. They were able to earn enough money to squeak out a living. It seemed like a high style of life in comparison to how they had been living.

In the spring (Feb or March1945), it was time to move on. They crossed Czechoslovakia into Austria under continual rain for days. My father found a triangular one-person tent made of goat hide and a pair of military boots on the side of the road. The boots were very big and both boots were for the same foot. My mother did not care and claimed the boots immediately because her feet were finally dry despite the fact they were walking in rain and mud both day and night. My father attached the tent so it covered the top of the wagon. It was the first time that Baby Lesya was truly protected from the rain and could breathe freely without her mother continually holding a stick under the canvas cover to let air in for the 12 month old baby to breath and not suffocate. My mother spent the whole journey on her knees in the wagon because there was no room to stretch her legs. My father walked on foot alongside the horses the whole journey through Ukraine, Poland, Czechoslovakia, Austria and Germany because the horses were so small and too weak to carry a heavier load.

Only God knows how this little entourage endured the travel challenges and weather elements without getting sick or killed. There were nights that they just lay on the ground under the wagons trying to fall asleep while getting drenched by the torrential rains. Baby Lesya always stayed dry under the little German canvas tent no matter how heavy the rain. As for her parents, they were like soaked puppies clustered together under the wagon.

As we crossed the foot hills in Austria, the rains were continual. The sun would peak out occasionally for at most an hour and then either the rain or snow would begin again. One day, the little caravan was caught for hours in an unexpected early spring snow storm with strong winds gusting and blinding them with snow. They kept moving trying to find shelter and finally saw a village in the distance, with a train station platform nearby. As the little caravan approached, they were stopped. They saw flat train cars loaded with wounded German soldiers. They were told that the military needed to use their wagons for the transport of the soldiers to a hospital in the village. The Germans loaded their wounded, all who were capable and coherent, on all of the available carts and wagons in the group. Rimsky's wife was told to drive one of the wagons that was loaded first. Her horses were skittish and slipping on the ice. The horses took off with the small wagon bouncing over bumps and piles of icy frozen soil as she tried desperately to control them. The wounded soldiers were screaming with pain using German expletives. She was told to keep going and not wait for the rest of us. By the time the rest of the wagons were loaded, we could no longer see her wagon. Once they reached the village and completed the transport, it was getting dark. They could not find Rymski's wife and no one had any idea what road she had taken. All the men set out in four directions searching for her on every village road and street. Her two little girls, sobbing for their mother, were left behind under my mother's care. Fortunately, their paths eventually crossed and everyone was joyfully reunited and at peace. They could finally put to rest the thoughts that no one could previously shake out of their minds…family members often could get separated permanently forever. It was one of the many horrific painful consequences of war.

This was their vagabond life – day and night -- on the road, always filled with worries and unexpected, unpleasant surprises. They heard the Russian military was advancing rapidly, so they continued to constantly move as quickly as possible. There was a real fear that the little caravan could accidently fall back behind the advancing Russian line, so there were no long stopovers to rest. Every day they arose up early, packed their supplies, fed the children and horses, and continued quickly on their way. They crossed Austria two days after the wounded soldiers' episode at the train station. They barely traveled into Germany a few miles when they encountered another unpleasant, dangerous surprise.

A group of young men called Ostarbeiters (German term for "Eastern workers") surrounded the wagons and confronted the little caravan on the road. Ostarbeiters (OST) were people from German occupied countries, that earlier in the war, had been deported against their will from their native countries to Germany as forced slave labor. They were treated very poorly by the Germans living on starvation rations in guarded labor camps. Totaling 3 to 5 million, they included both men and women and were mostly from the eastern countries of Ukraine, Poland, Belarus, and Russia.

The group of OST men spoke Russian and were armed. They were agitated with the little caravan of refugees, calling them names and accusing them of siding with the Germans. The husbands in the caravan first tried to reason with them; and then tried to convince the OST men that the caravan had gotten lost and now were looking for a way back home from Germany. The OST men did not really believe the story; but they did leave, brandishing their guns and threatening that if the caravan was caught again, everyone in it would be executed.

This was a dangerous situation NOT to be taken lightly. Previously when the Ostarbeiters had learned that the Germans had surrendered, they all walked off their jobs and formed gangs who robbed, looted and "payed back" the Germans for humiliating them as slaves. They did not discriminate so people who happened to fall into their path accidently (like the wagon caravans) was subject to similar treatment.

The wagon caravan families had travelled such a long treacherous road always looking forward to a future life of freedom. However, their hopes and dreams were becoming dashed with hopelessness. Fretting for their lives, their souls were filled with fear, not knowing what awaited them ahead and what next steps they should take.

After another full day of travel, they were afraid to stop in a village or town for fear of another encounter with other OST groups. Having reached a wooded area, the wagon caravan went deep into the woods, as far from the road as they could, and camped for the night in a small clearing. It was still quite cold with snow on the ground so the men built a fire in a large pit and put the wagons around it for protection and heat. There was no room on the wagons to sleep so the group huddled in blankets underneath the wagons trying to stay warm near the fire. They barely settled down when they heard machine gun fire in the distance. They were used to routinely hearing gun fire by now so they were not alarmed and hoped that it would be over soon.

Unfortunately, this time the shots kept coming closer and closer until some shots hit a wagon and some bounced off the metal on the wagon wheels. Everyone was terrified and jumped to run for cover deeper into the woods. The snow became much deeper as they ran. It was up to their knees in places. My mother had on the German men's boots both of the same foot, that we mentioned earlier. She kept slipping out of the boots and falling in the snow. My father took the baby from her so she could run more easily. She finally left the boots in the snow and ran barefoot to keep up with him. She remembered again why she had previously mentally made the decision to not run when they were caught in gunfire. They dug themselves into the brush and snow with teeth chattering trying not to move or make any noise. Finally, it became quiet. They all returned to the wagons. The men put the fire out in the pit and they sat huddled together in the cold and dark until the sun started to rise.

They decided to resume their travel by getting back to the road. They were stopped by a German soldier looking for civilian clothes; but they had nothing to give him because by now the clothes on their own backs were literally rags. We found out from the soldier that the territory was now controlled by American soldiers. As soon as the caravan left the forest and reached the road, it was completely surrounded by American jeeps. The soldiers had apparently been shooting into the forest all night thinking that there were German military hiding in the woods. The soldiers asked us who we were and where we were going. My father just told them that they were going to America. The soldiers laughed and exchanged some words among themselves, probably thinking "Good Luck! This is just the type of pilgrims America needs these days." The soldiers gave us some documents and directions to the next town and emphasized that we were not to go any further than that. Once in town, we were to find the military commander in charge and show him the documents. He then would find us food and shelter. We reached the German town of Neu-Ulm and did as we had been instructed. The military commander there was able to settle us into a building with metal grates in the window. It had previously housed French and Italian POWs. He gave us some German marks to get food and told the men in the group to come back the next day and he would give them work assignments with the local tradesmen and farmers. The men worked at various assigned jobs for money and the women set up house. Everyone tried to stay updated about the events of the war from the Germans living in the area.

It was May 5, 1945 and our new life began. Finally, we left our old way of life behind us. For the past two years, we had traveled by wagon in inclement weather, hid in the woods from crossfire, ran for cover from bombings, camped in abandoned buildings and forests. By the grace of God, the Neu-Ulm camp was on the Western side of Germany. At the time, we did not even comprehend how important that was and what it meant for our future destiny. Many of you reading may be too young to remember that Germany was divided into two parts after the WWII ended. The Eastern portion was controlled by the Soviets and the Western portion by the United States and Great Britain. God's big miracle of protection is that we arrived into the Western part of Germany without actually planning it. When my father decided to leave Ukraine, his only goal was to get out of communist territory which at that point could have been Germany or almost any country in Eastern Europe. He had no idea that after the peace treaty for WWII was signed, a whole block of Eastern European countries as well as Eastern Germany would come under Soviet rule. In fact, Germany itself would be divided: West Germany, the democratic side, would be controlled by NATO; East Germany, the communist side, would be controlled by the Soviet Union. But, God knew!

Does it make sense that the furnace, heated seven times more than what it was before, did not kill Daniel's friends? Not at all! The only reason they were alive was the presence of Jesus Christ with them.

In the Bible, Daniel says in Chapter 3;
"Then King Nebuchadnezzar was astonished and rose up in haste. He declared to his counselors, 'Did we not cast three men bound into the fire?'

They answered and said to the king, 'True, O king.' He answered and said, 'But I see four men unbound, walking in the midst of the fire, and they are not hurt; and the appearance of the fourth is like a son of the gods.'" Daniel 3:24-25.

Jesus Christ was with Sandra and her family and with many other refugees! This was not the end of the story! **(MN)**

Chapter 5 – Our New Life in the Refugee Camp

Being rescued in the river and spared from bombings in the war zone and landing on the western side of Germany were huge miracles experienced by the little caravan and that any person reading this can clearly acknowledge. But think about the accumulation of all God's little miracles that are missed unless you pause and think. Despite an unbelievable entrance into the world under unimaginable circumstances, I have never been seriously ill or in the hospital except to have my two children. I never had long-term health issues throughout my 80 years of life. That is not just amazing…it is a miracle and blessing from God once more.

We were unprotected, undernourished, pushed our bodies daily, exposed to harsh elements of weather, and even harsher and more dangerous elements of war. I was living on unpasteurized milk, chewed up chocolate, and whatever else my mother could chew up to give me. God wrapped us up in His divine protection during this whole journey.

God never stopped. God continued to provide --
even so much more than previously as we proceeded in
our journey to freedom. We settled comfortably into our
new life in the temporary refugee housing in Neu-Ulm but
it was not long before it brought some new challenges.

After some time, we started to get visitors
dropping in for pleasant conversation with us. They were
again Ostarbeiters (OSTs), the Ukrainians that had been
forcibly taken to Germany for manual labor from German
occupied territories when the Germans advanced into
Russia and neighboring countries. They were mostly
young men who were anxious to go back to the
homeland, and were a little too enthusiastic about inviting
us to join them. We were afraid to tell them the truth that
we were fleeing the homeland as they had plenty of
weapons and could have shot us. Secretly we were
afraid that they could be Soviet KGB, posing as
Ostarbeiters, whose directive was probably to collect
refugees and return them to the homeland.

God was even more involved in the details. After
the end of the war, the negotiations involved the three
great powers: Soviet Union, Britain and the United
States. Stalin negotiated with Roosevelt and Churchill to
allow all the people deported to Germany as forced
manual labor to be allowed to freely return home and he
would send trains to provide an easy transport back to
the homeland for them.

Stalin also convinced Churchill and Roosevelt that
the recent refugees had not really wanted to leave their

homeland; but rather had become displaced and unintentionally swept up in the military frontline as it moved west out of Ukraine. He wanted to give these people the same opportunity to come home. This sounds nice in a newspaper article or a press release but the reality was actually evil and quite the opposite. There was no oversight on the Allies part as they accepted the information in good faith and saw no reason to get involved in the refugee people "voluntarily" returning home. For my family, this "opportunity offered by Stalin" was a huge danger; and God once again delivered them with His hand of protection.

The visits from our newly found groups of "friends" became more frequent. They would show up to talk and reminisce with us about the homeland. They started to tell us about the trains that were coming to take them and other displaced people home. They became stronger in their encouragement for us to join them. Eventually, they started to schedule dates for people to move into their camp which was closer and more convenient to the train station while awaiting the arrival of the trains. These so called "friends" said, "You need to be ready to easily board the train when it comes to take you back to the homeland." These words did not appear as a kind offer of safe passage home. Rather, it felt like a death sentence. A command to return back to the very place you had risked your life to escape easily translated to torture and execution. There was so much anxiety spreading throughout the camp and there were rumors of mysterious disappearances and people who died by suicide. Death was easier to accept than the bondage of Stalin because the Ukrainian refugees knew definite execution awaited them upon return.

One day a group of young men came to where we lived and told our men that they and their families were scheduled to return to the homeland and needed to move to a closer camp. The families were so terrified that they could hardly breathe. Our men played along in agreement to whatever the young men communicated. My father knew that arguing would not help, so he expressed relief and great enthusiasm to these young men. He pretended to be very thankful that they had finally scheduled and arranged transport to the new camp for our little caravan group.

"Oh, I am so glad you have come. We have been trying to figure out a way to get home. Being caught up in the retreating military front line has been terrible, just terrible." said my father. He proceeded to explain to them that transporting our group with all the little children to the new camp might prove to be both challenging and emotionally disruptive. He wondered if they would agree to let all of them stay in place and just give them a few days advance notice before the train arrived. My father assured them that we would all arrive at the new camp in time to board the train. He finished the conversation by saying how excited he was to take his family back to Ukraine.

Certainly, this wasn't what the soldiers expected. They softened a little in silent victory and even allowed us about a week's extra time to pack and get ready. The soldiers left, telling us they would notify us on what day to be ready and would even come back with a truck to help transport our caravan and belongings to the train. I am not saying that God tells us to lie, but I am saying that God moved the soldiers to allow us to stay longer and not rush us.

My father knew returning for him was not an option. He understood people and he made plans to escape.

At this point a question crossed my mind: should Sandra's dad listen to that solider and expose his family to more danger and possible death, or should he save his family's life, even if it meant to telling a lie to that soldier? Well, people reading their Bible may remember what happened in Joshua's time where Rahab saved spies' lives by what she said. (Joshua 2:1-24). **(MN)**

And the Story continued!

My father and the other men took that week to roam the woods looking for a safe hiding place for us to camp and reside for a while. My family along with the other two families in the little caravan went deep into the woods and hid for over two weeks. During that time, my father occasionally slipped out stealthily to see if the trains transporting people back to the Soviet Union had departed. Finally, one day he was able to confirm with the Germans that the train convoy had left. Then, my father knew it was safe to take us out of hiding. We waited a few more days before we came back to our camp. When we returned, the people there said that the soldiers combed and ransacked the area looking for us.

God's protection of our little caravan was amazing. I'm grateful for what God did and the wisdom He gave my father. The Bible says, "A man's heart plans his ways but God directs his steps". Proverbs 16:9. What a living example of the truths of the Bible working in my family's life even before they knew Jesus.

In Mt 10:16-18, God reminds us that we are as helpless as sheep and we often find ourselves surrounded by ravenous wolves. He then says that we should be as wise as serpents, who express their wisdom in cunning ways. When such cunningness is exhibited by us who are as helpless as sheep, the combination is powerful. God uses our humility and weakness in combination with a cunning approach to provide a way of escape from a dangerous situation. Yuri Didenko was paying attention to internal, quiet messages of warning. We know that these messages come from the Holy Spirit, who cares for all of us, even though many do not pay attention to His voice. (MN)

Soon after, the temporary camp in Neu Ulm was closed and everyone was moved to a more permanent camp in Augsburg, Germany. This camp was formerly a group of military barracks where the Germans had housed and trained their soldiers. They were were long brick buildings, three stories high and placed around a paved public square. We were assigned Building 4, Room 38 on the third floor to share with two other families and two bachelors. Each family had a corner of the room for their living quarters separated by a curtain for privacy. The two bachelors shared the fourth corner together.

Now a longer permanence was established in our new life. For the families in the little caravan, living conditions were almost luxurious compare to what they had endured the past few years. Nevertheless, along with the benefits, the new way of life brought its own concerns and challenges, especially for people with little children. Lesya was almost two years old and needed to be watched constantly that she did not wander into other peoples' corners. People constantly moved and traded rooms as they made friends with whom they would rather live. Women competed for such things as standing in line for dinner rations or the use of the communal kitchen, signing up for bathing facilities, and rising at 4 AM to compete for laundry washtubs. Human nature was not at its best. Patience was in short supply and arguments would often break out. Gossip became an easy outlet to help vent emotions.

On the positive side, life had a way of reorganizing to a level of stability. Schools started opening for the children. An adult education program was established offering courses in languages like German and English as well as sewing and cooking classes for the women. There were courses for men in various trades that needed workers in the community thus offering better job opportunities. Soon even a church was established.

The biggest employer was the camp administration that hired men to cut firewood both for sale in the town and for the use of heating all the buildings in the camp. Unfortunately, the forest was quite far away so the men had to travel by train to work. They lived all week in a lumber camp in the forest and only came home on the weekends. This added a layer of loneliness to an already difficult existence.

It helped that people could sign up for garden plots to raise some of their own vegetables. Moreover, it provided a connection with the soil and land giving people a nostalgic comforting sense of home and memories of a life left behind. As a little escape from confines of the barracks, my mother and I spent many wonderful summer afternoons together as we planted, cared and harvested our little garden. There was also stables for some people that chose to still keep their horses and wagons from their journey. My father was one of those people so he still had 2 horses to care for. This provided a delightful, special treat for my little two year old heart as I loved going to feed them with my father.

Clothing was in short supply. It was hard to afford anything sold in the German stores on refugee earnings, especially when a lot of the economy was on a bartering system where the men traded working for food or supplies. There was a clothes closet in the camp for used clothing donated to the camp from various international humanitarian organizations. Most of the better clothes were picked out by the German camp administrators and other authorities before it reached the refugee closet area. By the time it was my mother's turn in the queue, it was very slim pickings when it came to clothes, especially in children's sizes. My mother tried to learn how to sew and knit from the older women. She became pretty creative and adaptive to taking apart clothes and altering them by hand to fit a child. An unexpected delight came from one of my father's bartering jobs. On some weekends my father worked for a farmer who paid him in rabbits and chickens which we killed and used as our weekly meat for a season. My father saved the rabbit skins and when he collected enough, he had them cured and found a seamstress to make me a little fur coat, with hat and muff to match. It ended up being my outer wardrobe when coming to America, easily making me stand out as a poster child for immigration.

After a year or so, people started leaving the refugee camp for other countries to start a new life. Initially people went to England, France and Belgium. Each country had their own quotas and work requirements. For example, Belgium was only taking people who were willing to work in the coal mines. Rumors started that Argentina and Australia were also going to start taking people but the quotas were very limited.

The Rhymski family were very cramped for living space in their corner of our room because they had two older children. They were the family who had traveled with us the longest on the wagon train journey through Eastern Europe and had become close friends. As people started leaving, there was more space available and they moved to another building. We did not see them as frequently; because there was little time in the day for social visits. We mostly just bumped into them in the public areas of the camp. One day they came to tell us that they had received their visas for Argentina. They had finished all their paperwork and were just waiting to know the date of their departure. This news was a shocking game changer for both families because for over three years, we had lived and traveled together through the thick and thin of life. We were in some ways a family, the only family we felt we had.

After they boarded their ship, life felt a little more empty and a little more somber. Building 4 Room 38 continued to be our home as we waited, hoping that God's affection and blessing would shine on us soon to give direction toward our new home and our future. The ending to our long journey felt so very close; and yet so far. There were so many unknowns that left us hanging in limbo. We knew that we would be leaving the camp in Germany eventually but when and to where? We had no choices for a final destination as yet. We didn't even know what part of the world this last leg of our journey would take us.

Finally, in late December 1948, a representative from the American Farm Bureau Association came to recruit workers for farms in the Maryland area. The camp loudspeaker announced that there would be a meeting in Building 2 the next afternoon for any men interested in farming to be interviewed. My father, both desperate and hopeful, went. He was a tall and well-built so easily caught the eye of the Bureau representative. He pointed at my father, called him over and asked if he had any experience in farming. Then he continued to ask about our family situation. The answers must have fit the profile that they were looking for because within a week's time, we had finished all the commissioned paper work; and were instructed to start packing.

A farmer from Maryland sponsored us to come to America. In return for paying the expense our voyage and supplying all living expenses for a year, my father had to work for the farmer for a year on his farm in Princess Anne, Maryland.

PART 3: New Country - New Home

Chapter 1 - Opportunity for a Fresh Start

On January 7, 1949, we boarded the ship called the Marine Flasher with sixty nine other people all looking toward to yet one final journey leading to a new life. Hopefully, this journey involving an ocean and a ship would be a little safer than the last journey by horse and wagon. I remember getting on this "huge" ship. My biggest problem was that Ukrainian Christmas was January 7th and I thought Saint Nicholas wasn't going to be able to find the ship. I remember crying that I would not get any presents. What could be worse than that for a four and a half year old little girl? Ah, but my life was going to get a lot worse just a day later.

My parents and I boarded the ship and found our living quarters. It was segregated with the men in separate quarters from the women. My mother and I found our room. There were bunk beds in it and I was sleeping on the top bunk. I distinctly remember that first night on the ship. It was horrifying. I awoke in the middle of the night to loud frightening sounds. I thought I heard animals or monsters roaring, and I was terrified by my own imagination. I was sure something awful was about to happen. Later, I discovered that the sounds were actually women getting seasick from the boat rocking in the rough ocean waves created by the harsh winter weather.

I cried out for my mother but she did not respond. She did not come to me. She was not there. A soft-spoken gentle woman finally came to hug me and say "Honey, it's okay. Go back to sleep. Your father will be here in the morning and you'll be alright." Every morning my father would come to the door of the women's quarters to pick me up. We would spend the whole day together and at night, he would bring me back to my sleeping quarters.

Typically, the public areas of the ship were fairly empty because so many people were seasick from the severe rocking of the boat. The weather was not suitable with any comfort or safety for walking or sitting outside on deck. Most of the eleven days at sea, you could not even walk inside the ship without holding on to something. At one point, the storms were so bad that the crew tied the table and chair legs together as one unit to keep them from sliding across the dining room floor.

I never saw my mom again for the entire eleven days that we were on the boat except one time toward the end of the voyage. My mother was so seasick that the crew had actually made a shelter of stacked deck chairs and a tarp on the deck so she could lay in a protected area outside to have fresh air. My father and some crew staff held onto me tightly as they took me outside to see her. I could feel the howling wind forcefully pushing against my little body. I was leaning as if I were a small tree that was resisting a massive blowing force that was pushing against it. I felt the stinging rain drops driven into my cold cheeks by the harsh wind like sharp little nails. I have this vivid image in black and white of my mother lying limp and very still. Her face was a shallow gray color and her body looked very frail. I am not sure whether I thought she was dead because a child that age may not be capable of such a thought. However, eight decades later, if I dwell on that moment today, my body can subconsciously experience the feelings of the shocking, traumatic conditions of that stormy day.

Remember, for the whole four and a half years, I had bonded intimately with my mother. My father was always preoccupied with navigating the challenges of our journey, the caring for the horses and the maintenance of the wagon. Initially he was driving the wagon. However most of our journey, he was walking next to the wagon to lighten the load for the horses. At the refugee camp, his work was a half day's train ride away so he was only home on weekends. Now being detachment from my mother totally shattered my security and I felt alone.

Later, years later, my mother asked if I remembered visiting her on the ship's deck in the storm. She told me that she didn't think she was going to survive the voyage and she wanted to see me one last time. She begged the crew to bring me out. They accommodated because they suspected that she might be right and wanted to honor her wishes.

111

When we finally arrived and docked in the Boston harbor, an ambulance was waiting to take my mother to the hospital. After a thorough checkup, she was treated for dehydration, and the doctors determined that she was well enough to travel again. She joined the rest of the ship's passengers on the final leg of their long journey traveling by train to Maryland. It felt safe and good to be reunited with my mother and father in a happy ending. However, the happy ending was short lived. Sometime after our train stop in Baltimore station, my mother began to feel ill again. Her condition became so severe that the conductor stopped the train at the next closest town. Again, she was taken by ambulance to the hospital while my father and I continued on in the train to Princess Anne, Maryland.

I wondered -- would I really ever see my mother again. I remember like it was yesterday. Once again, it was just my father and I. What was going on in my little child heart and mind? I do remember that last lonely part of the long train ride that ended with my father and I arriving at the farm. I have a vivid permanent image that is etched in my memory and heart. It was evening when we finally arrived in our new home in America. The sun was setting and there was an area of shallow water near the edge of the field -- a pond with

cattails. My father and I were standing on the shore looking across the pond and watching the last remnants of the sunset fade away. Being a big man, his 6' 2" build towered over me enveloping me in his shadow. I remember holding his hand and looking up at him. With my tiny little hand lost in his huge palm, I remember thinking to myself, "You're big, we will be okay because you're so big. You are going to keep me safe, and together we will all be just fine."

That's how our life started for me in America, the Land of Opportunity.

Reaching this part of the story, people could see a lot of Hallelujahs and praise God for all His protection going up in the air! Indeed, God was writing a story with Sandra's family. A story that will teach the love, the faithfulness, the protection, the provision of Yahweh! People can read this story and learn something new and amazing about the All-Mighty God. The One who came to rescue and save all those who will choose to welcome Him into their life. The only God who came to mankind as they were still sinners and lost. .... (MN)

Chapter 2 - Beginning Life in the Land of Opportunity

My mother joined us on the farm a few weeks later. Our little family was happily reunited once again. We were finally settling into a home and starting fresh!

Our new life started in a small little farmhouse that was sparsely furnished by most people's standards and an outhouse in the back yard. However, for us, it was amazing compared to what we had been experiencing during our journey over the past four plus years. After all, we had a solid roof over our heads that we could count on always keeping us dry. For us, sleeping on the floor on old mattresses was a luxury and the selection of mismatched dishes with random silverware was a delight. Can you imagine how blessed we felt, when a few weeks later, the farmer brought us a used bed? I could fill a whole chapter on adventures and surprises of immigrant life on the Maryland farm during that first year. These memories range from being awakened in the wee hours of the night because the cows that were sleeping in the pasture found a hole in the fence and were in the middle of the road blocking traffic to my mother once again being in the hospital when a random gust of wind blew fertilizer into her eyes while she was planting in the fields.

We spent the year working on the farm in Princess Anne to pay back Mr. Anderson, the farm owner, for our voyage. It had been a lot of hard work for both my mother and father; but they were grateful for their life on that farm. This new country offered so much more than they ever imagined, especially when compared to living under the oppression of communism.

Once the year was over, our commitment was fulfilled. Mr. Anderson tried to convince us to stay; but the language barrier and the dependence on him for every little thing was a lot to bear. My parents yearned to hear their heart language spoken. They missed community with people of their own ethnic background. Corresponding by mail with immigrant friends made them homesick for pieces of their birth culture that would preserve their memories of home. They knew that groups of Ukrainians refugees had begun to congregate and settle in Philadelphia. Friends living there kept encouraging my parents to come join them. They said that they did not have much; but what they had, they would share with us and we would all work it out together.

My parents had saved $500 out of the $25 per week salary that Mr. Anderson had been paying them. It was a huge risk and another big unknown. We packed what little we had, mostly food, clothes, and a few dishes that my mother had brought with her from Germany. It didn't take long to get ready. My parents' friends in Philadelphia knew an American man with a truck, who helped move immigrants as a second job. They made arrangements for him to come pick us up in Maryland and transport us to Philadelphia.

We lived with our friends – who encouraged us to move in-- for almost a month in their small four room apartment very snugly and frugally. It was bitter sweet. Reuniting with so many old friends that my parents knew from the refugee camp breathed joyous energy into my parents' social life, which was almost nonexistent in Maryland. Going to a Ukrainian Church, listening to the Orthodox mass in their native language for the first time in over a year fed their spiritual souls. Yet, the fear of running out of money before my father would find a job nagged on them constantly.

These were hard economic times throughout the United States in the early 1950s. Every day my father went from factory to factory looking for a job to no avail. My mother was 4 months pregnant so no one would even consider hiring her. One day, another friend from the German refugee camp told my father that there was a care taker position opening up where he was working on a farm as a horticultural gardener tending to flower beds. It was a 200 acres estate located about 45 minutes outside of Philadelphia and owned by Mrs. Scott, whose husband had started Scott Paper Company. The position was to oversee the farmed acreage of the estate and included a house to live in.

"Mrs. Scott was quite interested and wanted the whole family to come for the interview. The first hurdle was finding an interpreter, which she found through a local college. The interpreter was a kind, friendly man whose parents had immigrated to America after WWI. The interview went splendidly. The job description was to maintain the hay and corn fields by planting and harvesting corn and hay as feed for the animals. She had 2 horses and 4 cows that needed to be cared for, including milking the cows twice a day. She also wanted my father to plant and maintain a vegetable garden for her personal use. The job offer was $125 a month, a house to live in and all the milk from the evening milking (Mrs. Scott took the milk from the morning milking). We were so happy that we gratefully accepted whatever she offered.

Mrs. Scott seemed to like us almost instantly...I think her heart was touched by our childlike simplicity and courageous ability to persevere against all odds. She offered to pay the interpreter to oversee our move and get us settled. (As it turned out, we had so few belongings that he moved us in himself with his pickup truck.) Then she instructed the interpreter to go with Mrs. Paul, her estate manager, to show us our house which was at the edge of her estate surrounded by fields and a huge apple orchard. The house was old and had been neglected for a long time. It needed a lot of work; but to us, it felt like a seven room, two- story mansion.

We moved in around the end of October and Mrs. Scott dropped in to see us while we were moving. She asked the interpreter if he was going back to get the rest of our belongings. He told her this was all the belongings that we had: two suitcases, a bundle of bedding, a few dishes and a child. Mrs. Scott and the interpreter left soon after without saying much more. We, tired from the day's events, spread the bedding on the floor that may have been the empty living room and slept soundly in our large but empty new "mansion." We proudly called this home for the next twelve years until Mrs. Scott died at age eighty five.

Unbeknownst to us, Mrs. Scott had instructed Mrs. Paul, her administrative assistant and farm office manager, to go to the Salvation Army thrift stores and furnish our house with the basics. "A week later to our surprise, two beds, a couch, a cupboard, a dining table with 5 chairs and an old refrigerator arrived at our door. Overnight, we became rich and our "mansion" was filled with furniture. We carried our beds upstairs and set up 2 bedrooms…and our "royal life" began."*

* The above quoted section is translated from a personal memoir written by my mother.

Mrs. Scott would visit us couple times a month and we never knew why. Maybe she wanted to see how we were managing. She would look around, try to converse with us with a few words and hand gestures then quietly leave. Frequently, soon after her visits, gifts would arrive for the household or for me and my baby sister, Anne.

From a material point of view, life in America on Mrs. Scott's estate became more wonderful by the day. We experienced abundant changes in our life style almost weekly as people in the neighborhood heard about us and donated things that they no longer needed. Experiencing the amazing outflow of generosity, so unique to the American culture and its people, in turn gave us indescribable joy and peace in our hearts. My parents planted a big garden in the spring. They asked Mrs. Scott if they could buy some chickens to raise for eggs. She herself actually bought us 12 chickens and 2 little piglets with the agreement that we would provide her with eggs as she needed and we would raise the 2 piglets, one for her and one for us.

Is it not wonderful to observe that God's fingerprint and hospitality was in America's culture at the time? It is also true that many people laid down their lives to infuse God's values into America's culture. Those who know a little about the history of this nation will acknowledge these facts. Many founding fathers and some of their followers established this country on biblical principles like justice, freedom, liberty, and equality for all. The hospitality and generosity offered to Sandra and her family did not come from nowhere; but from God's principles infused into the culture and into people's core values. It is also true that every nation passes on to it's future generations the principles they believe in and hold dear in their heart. It is what parents try to teach their children even today by example. The question today is this: do we still have the same values in American culture and people's lives? The answer might be no. Therefore, the point here is that you and I have the responsibility to believe and to obey the only true God for the generations after us to benefit from freedom, mercy, generosity, and love. **(MN)**

My parents had always been concerned about me being left alone in this world without any living relatives close by when they passed away. My little sister Anne was born soon after we moved to Mrs. Scott's estate. Having a baby sister was a delightful added dimension to my life. My sister Barbara showed up two years later which created even more chaotic happiness and fun. Our little family of five Didenkos living in America was now complete. I would never again find myself alone. Our vegetable garden and little herd of farm animals provided food and meat for our family. With time, both were expanded somewhat to create a viable little farm where we sold and delivered produce and eggs to surrounding neighborhoods. Life was full. Life was complete and life was very good.

There were definite daily farm chores assigned to my sisters and me depending on our ages. Along with our responsibilities, we had many happy moments that came with farm living - climbing apple trees with my sisters to pick the first crispy ripe apple of the season; or in the summer, anxiously waiting for my father to come home from the fields to take us to the creek to swim as well as to bathe.

Nonetheless, other emotional adjustments remained challenges to overcome. I have flashbacks to that period of my childhood. When I entered kindergarten in the second half of that year, I did not know a word of English. I remember sitting on the floor with my back against the wall and my teacher Miss Finnegan came up to me. She looked at me and said something quietly as I stared back at her with big eyes in confused silence. Then, she bent down and smiled at me. She gently kissed me on the forehead, patted me on the head, and walked away. I don't remember anything else about that year but I must have learned some English. My next flash back of school was me entering first grade and saying to my first grade teacher, "Mrs. Putt, can you help me get all stars this year because I need a scholarship to college."

As in everyone's life, there are happy moments that when revisited, make you smile or giggle. Then, there are those difficult childhood memories that become foundational in building a portion of your adult character. As an adult, these are hard to process. You either try to stay away from these memories completely or you tread gently around them because they have the power to flood your soul with difficult and vivid emotions, as if they happened yesterday. Most of my memories were about not belonging and feeling heartbreakingly lonely. It was hard to fit in when the life style at home was so different from that of families who lived around you.

My parents had difficulty learning English. So from the start, I was the family translator for most adult situations such as doctors' visits, buying things in stores, and even doing taxes. At eight years old, I babysat my little sisters because my mother left to go to work in a factory as soon as I got home from school. I was responsible for the care of both Anne and Barbara, my toddler and my infant sisters. That included keeping the fire going in the wood burning stove in the kitchen for heat and cooking. My father came home towards evening to take over, after he had milked the cows and finished the evening farm chores. We were a team and I was part of the adult family dynamic that I gladly participated in to make life work.

As I look back, I realize that I missed some of the joys of simply being a child. Sometimes it feels like I skipped over that part of my life almost the way you skip a grade in school. I went right into being a little adult who was thrown into many aspects of adult life.

I so wanted my little sisters to feel American even though I knew I could not. I was keenly aware how different the lifestyle of my friends in the neighborhood was from my life on our little "Ukrainian" farm with chickens and pigs. I was determined to mimic the American style of life for my little sisters as close as I could.

I began babysitting for neighborhood families at an early age. This was especially true in the summer when mothers wanted someone to entertain their children because they needed to get something done or run errands. I always saved my babysitting money to buy my sisters things that they wanted whenever I could. For years when they were young, I played Santa Clause so they would be experience Christmas the way their friends did. Often those gifts would be the only Christmas presents that they would receive.

I felt like a person caught in two cultures and not fitting into either one very well. In full disclosure, most of those feelings were probably self-generated due to our immigrant lifestyle and circumstances rather than from children treating me poorly in school. We lived too far away for me to participate in any part of the Ukrainian community in Philadelphia; and our family dynamic was far too different from the middle class families that lived around us to even try to be like them. Life, of course, was hard on multiple levels but it also was VERY good in our eyes. We felt God's blessings in our souls. My parents needed me. We worked hard together and God provided abundantly.

In my adult life, I have experienced success in many spheres of my life and on many levels. Just as God provided when my mother birthed me in that cold barn during a freezing Ukrainian winter night, He has NEVER stopped being faithful in His provisions for me. God has showered me with blessings in my growing up years, through my long adult life, and now into my silver years. I am blessed materially, physically, and most of all, with a loving family and friends. My life has always been filled with many, many wonderful relationships. My friends are people from all places and all walks of life. Even my family members often play temporary roles acting as my friends when I ask them during a conversation to put their "friend hat" on to listen.

I need to model my contentment more frequently by following what my father often said to us. "Look at me. I am the most blessed man in the world having my life filled with true wealth. I have a truck and a car. I have a solid brick house. I have property with beautiful gardens and a fish pond all paid for........and best of all, my three daughters all have college educations; and I live in America, the Land of the Free. What else can a man ask for?" Those words ring in my ears often even today. Thankfully, it is where my spirit lives most of the time.

Yet, once in a while, an insatiable desire "to belong" can surface out of nowhere even today. It immerses me into a wave of feeling strangely alone and different from everyone. I know my feelings are not foreign to most of you readers. We each have experienced our own variety of childhood traumas. Sometimes it causes us to make childhood vows that we live out in our adult life unknowingly and unintentionally. I could write a whole other book on "feelings and experiences growing up as an immigrant child", but this is "my father's story".

My father was my rock ever since that first evening at our little farm house in Maryland when we watched the sun set over the pond together with his big hand totally enveloping mine. He was the wind beneath my wings that helped me through the trying experiences of my early childhood and school years.

He came to America in the prime of his life at forty years old, with 2 suitcases, a sick wife, a 4 year old child, and not knowing a word of English. My father must have felt it would be impossible to fulfill his personal dreams and ambitions. I envision him having his own personal experience as he stood with me on the shore of that same pond and watching the same sunset on the evening we arrived at the Maryland farm. As he pondered his situation of unfulfilled dreams, he might have looked down and decided to pour them all into this 4 year old little girl holding his hand standing next to him. After all, why not test the American dream of "Being the Land of Opportunity ".

I think that is where my request to my first grade teacher originated. A lot of times when I came home from school, I went to find my father plowing in the field. Sometimes it was because I came home crying; and I wanted tell him about something sad that had happened to me socially that really hurt my feelings. Other times I wanted to share something that would please him such as a high test grade or an achievement award. Those latter times were extra precious because he would tear up as he listened or I showed him the test paper. After a while, I lived to make my father cry. Those trips to the corn or hay fields were very special because I knew one of us would be crying...I loved it when the tears were his; and he had an uncanny ability to comfort me when they were mine.

Each of those conversations in the field always finished with the same parting comment. "Honey, the streets in America are made of gold. They're just under a lot of dirt. You're going to have to dig deep and work very hard. You will need a shovel to dig; and that shovel is a scholarship for college. Work hard to achieve something and the day will come where you will gain the respect of people. Then everyone will want to be your "friend".

That was the mantra that he repeated during my whole childhood, etching these words deep within my heart. It served me well in life as I got to choose from several scholarships to various colleges. I went to the University of Rochester where I met and later married my college sweetheart. We both have been amazingly fulfilled and successful in our chosen careers while balancing parenthood in the process. We raised two wonderful daughters in a delightfully close family environment that still exists today. They both married wonderful, caring men and expanded our family to include six fun loving grandchildren.

Yes, my life could be a poster story for the American Success Story.

Many people can relate to it not being easy, to go away from your home, and country to live in a new place and culture that is not yours! People usually face the question of identity, and who they are in that context. This challenge is not new to many missionary families who leave their nations to serve the Lord in other cultures. There are 3 to 4 different groups of people who leave their homeland.

1) *The first group is those who are forced to leave their nation because of wars or other dangers. They usually look for a place of safety and refuge. They work hard to build a new identity in a new culture.*
2) *The second group is people who freely leave their nation to seek a better life. They are usually people who choose to become immigrants in a nation that will provide freedom, financial prosperity, good education, and wealth. These are nations that have God's principles in their culture. Justice, love, mercy,*

wealth, science, and technology come from the only true God

3) *The third group is people sent by their governments to work in other countries. They are usually strong in their home identity and feel free to either integrate into the new culture or not.*

4) *The last group is the group of people who leave their homes, and their countries, in obedience to God, to serve people in other parts of the world and teach them the ways of God.*

Jesus Christ, the son of God, went far away from heaven, to die on the cross in this broken world so that everyone who receives Him in their lives should be forgiven for their sins and have everlasting life. Because God loves us so much, He decided to make a way, to give everyone the possibility of having a new life, hope, and a new home. Everyone who believes in Christ becomes a new creation and God gives to that person a new heart and identity that will not change no matter where they live. The Bible says: "So then you are no longer strangers and aliens, but you are fellow citizens with the saints and members of the house of God.... In Him, you also are being built together into a dwelling place for God by his Spirit." Ephesians 2: 19-22.

*To become a son or a daughter in Christ Jesus matters more than anything else. Then God gives you the best identity, future, family, and home ever! **(MN)***

Chapter 3 – Living Life with Mrs. Scott

Time passed and for eleven years, life truly began to feel more settled with fewer and fewer bumps and challenges. My parents still worked very hard work, but their rewards were great. Our house was equipped with all the amenities of a middle class American home. My parents had both become American citizens. They were very proud of this accomplishment because they had to study hard to pass the test in English. Later, they became fluent enough in English to feel their way through any normal conversation that might be needed in daily life. They were quite independent as they owned both a truck and a car and both had their driver's licenses.

As with everyone's life, there were happy surprises and some sad life changing events. One of the kindest and happiest events for our family involved Mrs. Scott. She was, and continues to be, our family's role model of America's kind and extremely generous heart to people in need.

Mrs. Scott really enjoyed my father and his happily, content personality. My father had a wonderful strong tenor voice and loved to sing. As I had previously mentioned he was a happy man who always chose to feel emotional abundance rather than emotional scarcity. From childhood he loved tilling the land. Most of his days consisted of working the fields on a tractor singing his heart out with his favorite Ukrainian songs that were heard easily across the acres of corn and hay fields. Mrs. Scott once told me that sometimes she would come out and sit in her flower gardens just to hear him sing because it lifted her spirits.

One summer day in 1958, she told my father not to come to work the next day but to be ready for Walter, the chauffer, to pick him up because they needed to go into town. She asked my father to bring me along to translate. He, of course, obliged without questioning. We were ready and waiting the next morning when Walter and Mrs. Scott arrived in her long black Cadillac and drove us to the county courthouse in Media. On the way, she tried to explain to my father as I translated that she was getting old. She said that she was concerned what would happen to him and our family when she passed away. She said that she had an acre of land surveyed and subdivided into two half acre parcels from her estate. Now she was bringing my father to the courthouse to sign some papers. She was not giving enough details for me to understand and translate well so my father and I went along with whatever the plan was. Inside the courthouse, the clerk had my father sign the papers and then he asked my father to pay a dollar to finish the transaction. The transaction was completed and we left.

After we got back into the car, Mrs. Scott told my father that he now owned one acre of America!!! She took a dollar out of her pocketbook and gave it back to him. After we drove home, Mrs. Scott showed my father the designated ribboned stakes outlining the acre property. It was right next to the house where we lived. Then she gave my father explicit instructions that upon her death, he was to take that acre of land that was divided in half and sell one of the half acre of the land. Then, he was to use the money from that sale to build our family a house on the remaining half acre. She continued to say that there was an Arthur Hoyt Scott Horticultural Center in Swarthmore College that she had created in honor of her late husband in 1929 and it was funded by The Scott Foundation. (Mrs. Scott and her husband had met and graduated from Swarthmore College). She said that upon her death, my father automatically had a job at the Center as a gardener for as long as he wanted. She also said that her estate would most likely be sold and turned into a neighborhood development after her death. Her intention was that our family would have a place to live and that he would have a place to work for as long as it made him happy to do so.

Mrs. Scott died in 1960 at the age of 85. Her wishes were carried out to the last detail as per her instructions to my father. He sold his little half acre of land and used that money toward building a modest three-bedroom red brick ranch house on the remaining half acre. He found a man in his group of Ukrainian refuge friends who was a builder in Ukraine and then had been working in the building trade for eleven years since he arrived in America. My father and the builder did the hard labor of building the house while hiring contractors to do the things that they were not licensed to do or could not do. It took almost two years to build the house with my parents doing most of the inside work with their own hands.

In fall of 1962 when I went away to college, I left from the house that Mrs. Scott had originally provided for our family twelve years earlier. I returned home, the following spring after my freshman year, to a new house located on the edge of a neighborhood. A large builder had bought the Scott estate and there was already little glimpses of future development happening around us and our little farm was slowly becoming just a sweet memory from an era gone by.

My father worked for the Scott Horticultural Gardens in Swarthmore College for another 15 years until he retired. He lived in the little brick ranch house that Mrs. Scott so generously provided until his death at 89 years old. In his retirement years, he would "farm" his large vegetable garden, tend to his landscaping and flowers, and spend lazy summer afternoons sitting by his fishpond – the one he had dug out with his own hands from a fresh spring that was on the property. It even had a sign nailed on a nearby tree saying "NO Fishing". (*I think Mrs. Scott was pleased and smiling.*)

My parents had worked so hard all their lives. Once they were retired, I wanted them to travel with us on vacations to enjoy other places in America and abroad. Every time I tried to earnestly invite them to go with us on a trip, my father would look at me and smile. His answer was always the same. "Where else could I travel that would be as peaceful and beautiful as this place, my home? Look at my fish pond. Look at my flowering gardens," he would say. Once with a twinkle in his eye, he said, "Lesya, Honey, I have seen half the world close up and personal in my lifetime, so you go see the other half for me; and together we will have covered the whole earth."

However, little did I know that deep in his heart, there was one more trip that he yearned to take and he lived long enough to have God provide it. That is the final chapter of this whole story.

Chapter 4 - My Father's Journey to Faith

After college, Bob and I got married and moved to Penn State University for him to pursue a PhD graduate program in computer science. It was an interesting life that included all the challenges that married graduate students face and all the wonderful crazy adventures that young married couples willingly indulge in despite some risks. In the quiet of an evening's end or relaxing on a lazy summer afternoon, Bob and I have sometimes reflect back and ponder the choices we made as we navigated our early married life together. You know those choices where the road ends with two bends either right or left; but you only get to go down one of the bends? You wrestle with the choice, knowing whatever bend you choose, that path will lead you to a different future life than if you had chosen the other bend. It is a fun mental exercise to ponder about "the road not taken" in our past and wonder where our life would be now if we had actually chosen "the road not taken" at those crossroads.

The choice leading to Penn State is one that we rarely ponder in a serious fashion as it was where the seed was planted for me to go to dental school which was a life changing decision. Even more important, Penn State is where the start of a life changing spiritual journey began for both Bob and me.

A college student approached me on campus one day and invited me to take a survey about God. The conversation was about how to have an assurance of going to heaven when you die as well as how to have a personal relationship with a living God right now through His Son Jesus to guide you in your daily life through prayer and dependence on Him. She invited me to attend a meeting of a student group on campus called Cru to learn more.

Bob and I both came from church attending families and ascribed to the religious beliefs of the mainstream Christian churches and the Bible. We maintained all those beliefs and attended church in our adult life together. However, a personal relationship with a loving God who wanted to walk with you here on earth was fascinating to me. Bob was more skeptical, but was willing to attend the meeting so we could be together. That evening meeting was the beginning of almost a two-year journey as we learned more about this personal faith and the saving grace of Jesus Christ dying on the cross for us personally. It is different from formal religion. This new life was obtained by a simple prayer, confessing to be a sinner, acknowledging that God sent His Son Jesus Christ to die on the cross for my sins, and inviting Him into my heart as the guiding Lord of my life personally.

This message is hugely complex and yet, a simple concept to absorb. However, when it actually sinks deep into your heart, your life and how you live it changes forever. When this spiritual life-changing event happens in a person's heart, the one of the first thing they want to do is to share this Good News with the people closest to them. I was no different and my father was at the top of my list.

The next time that Bob and I went to visit my parents, I found time to be with my father alone and I presented my newly discovered belief system with great earnestness; but with some verbal awkwardness as I discovered how much my Ukrainian vocabulary lacked the spiritual words that were so common in my English vocabulary. He listened respectfully but had no real response. I was left disappointed, fully blaming my lack of success on my poor presentation. I vowed to get better in my presentation and expand the spiritual portion of my Ukrainian vocabulary.

Over a period of 20 years, I tried earnestly two more times to present the Biblical gospel message to my father. Every time I tried, the conversation ended in a respectful silence. Finally, on my last attempt, my father listened to me intently and then said, "Daughter." (I knew it was serious because he addressed me as "daughter" only when I was in trouble.) He continued, "Daughter, I have something to tell you. Your great grandfather was Ukrainian Orthodox, your grandfather was Ukrainian

Orthodox, your father is Ukrainian Orthodox, and you are Ukrainian Orthodox no matter what you think you are." Leaving me speechless, he walked away.

I never attempted to bring up the subject to my father again. Some time after my last attempt to have a spiritual conversation with my father, my mother came alone to our house to babysit our daughters while we went on a trip. Bob had an opportunity to present the gospel message to her and to our delight, she understood. By then, I had given up and no longer gave any thought of involving my father in the topic again.

Every year our church performed an Easter cantata program giving church members an opportunity to invite friends. Bob loved to sing and actively participated every year in the cantata performance. He has a beautiful baritone voice; and one year in the late 80's, he had an especially important lead role. My father loved music; and as you remember, he himself loved to sing. He wanted to hear Bob sing and had decided to drive down for the Saturday night performance.

The previous day, on Friday, I was driving home from work mentally deciding the menus for the weekend, when my mind drifted to the cantata and its story. Suddenly, I was overcome by a vision of me dying and going to heaven; and my father not being there. I was overwhelmed with horror, choking with sobs and so flooded with tears that I literally could not see to drive. I pulled over into a side street and sobbed until I was totally drained physically. With my last sob, I screamed to God with an ultimatum saying, "God, if my father is not going to be in heaven I do NOT want to be there either. I don't care, God, I am not coming, despite Your guarantee of a place for me in heaven." And then, there was a silent stillness both in the air and in my drained body. I sat motionless fully expecting either to hear a thundering Voice or for lightening to strike the car. Neither happened. I sat there in stillness until I could pull myself together enough to drive. Fortunately, no one was home; and I did not say anything to anybody about my little "talk" with God.

My father arrived Saturday afternoon to go to the cantata. He was about 79 years old and had lived in America 40 years now. He knew English well enough to get by in his daily life; but I was not sure how much of the plot details he would understand about the story in the Easter Cantata. However, I did know that no matter what the plot was, the same scene always appeared of Jesus stumbling under the weight of the heavy wooden cross down the left center aisle of the church with loud cracking whipping sounds coming out of the front speakers as the soldiers pretended to crack their whips on his bleeding back. For the sake of my father understanding the details of the plot, the "human" in me knew exactly where I needed to find seats for us at the performance. I made sure we got there early enough to have a good selection of seats. I found two seats in a pew right smack on the aisle that Jesus would be coming down and sat my father on the end seat. That way my father would hear the loud cracking sounds of the whip sounds for a while as a buildup to getting a full view of Jesus bleeding, as the person playing Jesus stumbled weakly down the aisle to the stage, climaxing in a full crucifixion that looked VERY real.

The performance was captivating. At the end, the pastor gave an invitation to God's gospel message and instructions to fill out a card so someone from the church could follow up with more information. We left the church in silence; but driving home, my father quietly asked, "Lesya, Was it really that bad and painful with all that torture?" And then God spoke through me. I said, "Tato, it was not the physical pain that caused the suffering. You know that even humans can suffer great physical pain. You certainly did in your life. Years ago, I remember an incident up close and personal when you had your cut toe stitched up without anesthesia because you did not want the doctor to inject any anesthetic "poison" in your body. Physical pain is something even we human beings can bear. The pain that Jesus was feeling was different. It was the excruciating weight of the sin of the whole world; and it was not the general sin of the world as you might think. It was the personal sin of each individual person. It was your sin. It was my sin. He willingly took all that upon Himself to suffer and die. He loved you that much."

We rode home the rest of the way in a peaceful silence. I think for the first time, my father pondered the gravity of the story that I had told him several times in the past. When we got home, life continued in its usual evening routine. He sat quietly on the loveseat in the kitchen as I prepared food for the next day's meals.

Sometime later, Bob came home and with great excitement, started to tell me about the astounding number of people that had checked the box on the invitation card saying that they had prayed to accept the Lord after hearing the salvation message from the pastor. I will never know how or why these words came out of my mouth except I think there was a fourth person in that kitchen whose presence we were not aware of. I said, "Don't tell me. Tell him." And I pointed to my father still sitting on the couch.

Bob turned and said, 'Tato, come here I want to show you something." He then pulled out his blank invitation card and started to explain what it was for. I stood back incredulous in silence with my heart pounding. You have to understand that despite living in America for about forty years, my father probably only knew about 500 words in English. Bob, being married to me for about 20 years, knew about 200 words in Ukrainian. I stood watching in disbelief as the two most important men in my life were standing at my kitchen island having an intentional conversation about the most important topic in life, the salvation message, and actually understanding each other despite severe language barriers. I remained silent except for occasionally translating a word if one of the got stuck. However, it was pretty clear that there was another translator in the room that we did not see.

The conversation was coming to a close, and then it happened. As Bob finished explaining about the boxes to check on the card, he pushed the card closer toward my father. He then said, "Tato, do you want to sign the card?" My father looked at him straight in the eye and replied, "Give me a pencil" … and Bob did. I still have that card today. Whenever I see that card or think about that evening, I thank God for not only overlooking my "2 year-old tantrum" that I had thrown, but mercifully honoring my desperate prayer in the car parked on the side of the road.

Chapter 5 - Taking My Father Back to His Roots

During the few next years after Bob and my father had their spiritual conversation, I occasionally pushed God for signs of assurance that my father really understood what he did symbolically when he checked the box and signed that card. The USSR was still strongly intact and ruled by President Mikhail Gorbachev. Ukraine was still under Soviet rule with Russian as the official language being taught in their schools. It was hard to get any literature written in Ukrainian let alone a Bible. Understandably, my father's feelings were beyond negative when it came to anything involving Russian, especially pertaining to language and culture. There was no way he would be convinced to read anything in Russian no matter what it was; and of course, Bibles written in Ukrainian were few and far between. We eventually were able to get one for my father. I will confess in my weaker moments, I questioned privately to myself whether he really knew the significance of what he had done on that precious night. Was he even reading the Bible that we had found especially for him?

I know how I deeply wanted to believe it in my heart; and then one day, God sweetly squelched the remnants of my doubts. When we were visiting my parents one time, my father called me down to his fish pond where he typically spent many peaceful and contented hours. He loved his pond. He said, "Lesya, I have a question I want to ask you. Did you know Jesus was a Jew?" He continued, "I was so surprised, I had to ask the priest in church about it." I smiled as I answered him; and thought to myself, "Well, my father must be reading the Bible we gave him; and now it is up to God to make sure that he clearly understands the message."

In 1991, the Soviet Union crumbled and on August 24th Ukraine became its own democratic country free from Russian rule. It was a glorious day for my father as I don't think he believed that day would ever come. Very soon after that, my father invited me back to the fish pond for another serious conversation. He said, Lesya, my country is finally free and a sovereign nation. I yearn to "hold that rich black soil in my hands just one more time." Can you possibly take me back to Ukraine just for one visit? I teared up knowing, there was only one answer.

My sweet husband instantly agreed when I told him about the conversation at the pond. It became a pilgrimage of "many firsts" that we will always cherish and never forget.

We would finally see that amazing, peaceful green countryside scattered with poppies and sunflowers that I had heard about in so many stories as a child and then passed on to my husband and children. I myself yearned to focus my eyes on the rolling yellow wheat fields stretching all the way to the horizon; and to walk through the tall pine forests reaching to the sky. Most of all, I would finally meet my extended family of cousins, aunts and uncles that I had yearned to know over all these years. (Growing up having only a nuclear family of five Didenkos in America had been one of the main painful things that set me aside as different from my friends, especially on holidays.)

However, the biggest blessing of our family visit to Ukraine was observing firsthand the "harvests" of my father's faith journey. It started on the plane flying over to Ukraine in May 1992. Somewhere over the middle of the Atlantic Ocean, my father, sitting next to me on the plane, pulled out a small well aged black and white photo of a pretty young woman with a little girl sitting on her lap. He started to tell me that he had been married before and had a little girl with that marriage. His first wife had died of tuberculosis when the child was very small. Before his wife died, she made my father promise that he would let her mother, who was living with them, raise their little girl which he did.

When he was forced to leave Ukraine many years ago, he left a small tender part of himself behind. Now that he was going back to Ukraine, he wanted to try to find her and hoped God would help him. It was a lot for me to personally absorb and process, but I was anxious to help him in the search.

When we arrived at Boryspil International Airport we had 14 huge boxes of clothing and gifts for all our relatives, each box weighting 70 pounds. I knew they had so little, so I was anxious to bring as much over as I could by taking advantage to maximize the airline baggage weight allotment and even paying a little more for the overweight. For many weeks prior to our trip, I selectively decluttering all the bedrooms and toy closets until they were almost empty. I bribed my children to give up some of their toys. I asked friends and neighbors to donate from their closets. After that I shopped, and shopped, and then shopped some more. Every member of the family actively participated to the point that on a beautiful warm spring day, we all boarded the plane wearing double layers of sweaters, jackets and coats that we planned to give away. However, all the energetic activity in preparation was nothing compared to the energy and activity that was waiting for us when we landed in Ukraine.

As we exited the plane, there were 75 to 100 people with bouquets of flowers in their hands waiting to greet my father and meet us. There were relatives from both sides of the family who came from several different villages as well as the cities of Kiev and Odessa. I am sure other passengers on the plane thought there had been some international dignitary on the plane with them. The relatives from Yasnozir'ya rented a bus from the village center to pick us up. Yasnozir'ya, as you might remember from the beginning of the story, is where my father last worked, and from where they left when my mother made the decision to leave with my father to escape communism. My mother was born and grew up there. It was where they met and lived after they were married. It was HOME and we all felt the love and sense of belonging. It was our home base for the next 3 weeks as we traveled to see family members living in other parts of the country.

Let me tell you a little about our little village of Yasnozir'ya. As you approached the village, depending on which of its three bumpy roads you were traveling, you are surrounded by vistas of rolling fields (called steppe) of wheat, sunflowers, or poppies for miles as far as the eye could see. Occasionally, a row of tall thin poplar trees will appear almost as if to provide a border to the expansive fields. In some areas, the rolling fields are replaced with tall pine forests reaching to the skies for a change of scenery. Nestled peacefully among all this natural beauty is a little bucolic village where inside, a bustling industrious group of people carve out a modest living for themselves and their families from the rich earth that they call home. Most of them are born there, live their whole life there and die right within the boundaries of the village.

It was a delightful little place made up of winding dirt roads and thatched roof houses with charming gardens with vibrant colored flowers in the front yards. Most families owned enough surrounding land around the house to create little farms. Each had a small barn with a few cows supplying milk, chickens running in the barn yard, a few piglets being raised for meat, and huge vegetable gardens and hay fields in the back. There were community pastures were children took the cows to graze for the day in the summers. As soon as children could walk and talk, they were assigned chores according to age. The older sibling functioned as a babysitter while the younger followed an older around in an apprentice training role. Each house still had a functioning well on the property but most of the families had running water in their houses. However, indoor toilets were something progress still had not yet provided. There were a lot of these small villages across the rural plains of Ukraine. The villages appeared as if they had frozen in time as the rest of the world continued to westernize.

The evening when we arrived, a welcome dinner was planned at one of the wealthier cousin's house. He was the village veterinarian with obviously a huge guaranteed client base. It was a big house by their standards. My cousin had just finished building an indoor bathroom with a toilet that he rushed to finish in honor of the "American relatives" coming to visit. As you walked into the hall at the front door, the bathroom was uniquely positioned for easy viewing on the left-hand side. Interestingly, the top third of the door to the bathroom was frosted glass so it was easy to admire the inside. The toilet flushing was ingenious. There was a hose hung from the ceiling to fill the tub with water; but when you held the hose over the toilet bowl, it served to flush the water in the toilet.

The dinner table, consisting of several tables put together end to end, extended through two adjoining rooms. It felt as if almost the whole village had been invited to dinner in order to meet and greet us. They placed my father at the head table with us next to him on one side. Remember, earlier in my story when my father appeared bigger than life to the "four year old" me watching the sunset? Well, forty years later, a hint of that same presence and stature appeared again at the head of the table. I watched my father with a glow of peaceful joy on his smiling face as his eyes surveyed the room. I thought I saw his chest rise slightly as if his heart had filled to such overflowing that it was about to burst with pride and overwhelming gratitude. This was a man that was back in his native country, back with his people and back in his element. My father was HOME again.

In Slavic and Ukrainian fashion, the first thing that happens at any big celebration is a toast to the guest of honor with shots of homemade moonshine. This once in-a-life-time event was no different. As the fifty or more people raised their full shot glasses toward my father, someone said, "Yura, we need to toast to your good health and your coming home as our hero." Then suddenly my father's face turned quietly serious as he sat up a little straighter in his chair with his hand extended almost in a blessing manner and started to speak. He said, "My dear relatives, my countrymen and close friends, you know how much I love you and treasure my Ukraine, her culture and our people. I was born in this dear country. My afterbirth is buried in her rich soil. The best years of my life were growing up on her steppes and rolling wheat fields; and when I had to go, I left my heart behind. So you all know where my heart and patriotism continue to abide. However, I now have a new adopted country. That generous country opened its arms when my family and I had nothing and needed a home. Its people are warm, kind and have their own wonderful traditions. In my adopted country, we thank God for our food before we toast and my son Bob will thank God for the food and then we can continue with the toast.

Poor Bob, through this whole day between the handful of words he knew in Ukrainian and my sporadic attempts to translate for him, he gallantly attempted to capture the gist of conversations. By now his brain was tired; and most of the time, his mind reverted to daydreaming as an escape. However, it quickly lurched back to the present when his ears picked up the only familiar sounding word in my father's speech, which was my father's Ukrainian pronunciation of his name "Bohhb". I leaned over to him and quickly translated what my father had been saying. After a moment of incredulous confusion, we had a plan. "Bohhb" stood up and thanked God for the food in a very special extended prayer pausing several times so I could translate.... and then they raised their glasses for the toast while Bob and I prayed that his words would find their way into their hearts.

A most amazing thing began to occur and continued repeatedly through our whole visit. Whenever everyone sat down to eat, one of the Ukrainian relatives would say, "Bohhb, please thank God for our food so we can toast." We prayed in a similar manner every time. Their desire to incorporate this routine at the beginning of every meal was a delightful surprise and a blessing for us. We left the rest in God's hands.

The remaining three weeks were consumed with local travel. It quickly became clear, that my father returned to his home country with an intentional game plan in mind. It was a continuing daily process of delightful discoveries navigated by my father's personal goals/desires for this, his momentous trip. It got to the point that rather than questioning him about the day's itinerary, we just got in the car in the morning and followed expectantly to see what adventure the day had in store for us. More often than not, a story would unfold unexpectedly before our eyes; and our recourse was to quietly step back and watch with awe. Volodya, the veterinarian, appointed himself to be the designated "Uber driver" available at my father's disposable to go at any time to any place he desired. My father definitely had a mental map that he was using in his head. Some of the places were predictable because relatives from other places in the country had shown up at the airport. However, most of the places were surprises that had a connected story as to why we were going to try to find these people.

First order of business was to search for Olya, the "little girl with her mother" in the picture that my father showed me in the plane flying to Ukraine. We went to the town where he and his first wife had lived as a family; and the house where my father had last left Olya living with her maternal grandmother. This was the home where my father last said goodbye to her, knowing he was going to leave the country. There was no one at house when we knocked on the door and looked around the yard.

A neighbor lady across the street was standing in her front yard watching intently. As my father approached her, she cried out in total disbelief, "Yura Didenko, it can NOT be you!" In the nostalgic recalling of memories from long ago which followed, she happened to mention how good looking he was in his youth. We found out that Olya had indeed been raised by her grandmother into adulthood and had become a teacher. She had moved quite a few years ago to another town about 20 miles away that she named but knew nothing else about her.

We set out to that town, and there were able to locate the neighborhood where she lived. We stopped a woman on the street in the neighborhood, who confirmed that indeed, Olya lived in the area and actually had been her daughter's teacher last year. She called her daughter over and asked her to take us to Olya's house because giving directions would be too complicated. Even in our country's calmer times as in the mid 90's, I don't think many of us would have let our child get in the car with total strangers, especially since Volodya was the only one that even looked Ukrainian. My personal thought is that values often track with growth and progress in a culture. Since there essentially was no significant modern Western changes in Ukraine for years, the values also remained unchanged in a positive trusting way. We drove through several winding streets until the little girl cried, "There she is walking toward us."

Our hearts stopped. The little girl jumped out of the car and ran home as we all sat frozen in silence looking ahead where she had pointed. It felt like an eternity before my father started to get out of the car instructing us to all sit there. He began to slowly walk toward her. You can imagine the emotions being experienced by my father as he approached his "lost" daughter. This was one of those special surprises connected to an already amazing story. To do it justice, it would take a whole other book to describe in detail the continuation of the reunion. Many happy years followed as we kept in touch and visited in both directions.

Suffice it to say, when Olya finally truly comprehended that her birth father was standing right in front of her after all those years, there were overflowing emotions and an unending flood of tears. A final story is worth mentioning here because it illustrates the power of prayer and God's unending love interwoven into the details of our personal lives.

Olya said that her grandmother always described her father as a generous, kind and loving who loved her very much. She told Olya when he said good bye that last time to try to escape the country, he told her grandmother that if he survived that he would come back to get them. Her grandmother told Olya that her father was a man of his word; and if he was still alive, she could count on him coming back to find her. Olya said that all her life, her grandmother and she lit a candle in church every Easter and prayed that he was alive. She also said that after her grandmother died, she continued the tradition faithfully... always lighting a candle at Easter and praying for her father's return. Finally, at Easter just last year, she did the math and realized that over 40 years had passed. Believing her grandmother, she decided that he must have died in the war trying to escape and did not light a candle for him that past Easter. As much as I would love to linger with you in the emotion of the moment in this story, I have other places to take you and other stories to tell before I can finish this book.

As my father's story unfolded further, apparently, he married a second time right when the Germans were invading Ukraine in their effort to take over Russia. My father was away on business when the military front moved dangerously close. The village where they lived came under attack and my father could not get back. His father-in-law held a high position in the village and had an opportunity to leave in order to escape the danger. He insisted on taking his daughter and newborn baby granddaughter with him. Life in those days felt very unsettled with potential risk and danger around every corner. When my father finally was able to return home to the village months later, he found an empty house surrounded by destruction. When he started to search for them, the neighbors said that all three had perished while crossing a river as they tried to escape.

In our daily travels and asking local people in the area, another version of the story surfaced. Apparently only his wife's father was killed. His wife and child had survived but did not return to the village after the war was over. Through further word of mouth searching, we were told that his wife had passed away several years ago; but Vera, his daughter, was still alive, and lived in Kharkov quite a long distance away. However, she was known to spend summers in a village just an hour away from Yasnozir'ya, where her aunt had left her a small dacha (cottage). One more ride and a little more searching culminated in another tearful, emotional reunion. This time, it was in a vegetable garden where we found Vera weeding.

God was answering my childhood yearnings for a bigger family of Didenko siblings and a more expansive family. God is a wonderful steward to create secondary ripples whether around blessings or trials. During our visit, we were able to unite Olya and Vera together, both of whom were delighted with the discovery of an existing half sister as they were both only children. The extension of this sweet story is that Vera and her family moved from Kharkov to Cherkassy to be closer to Olya and her family. Happily, Cherkassy is also the closest real city to Yasnozir'ya. Talk about God taking tragic pieces of life and in His timing putting them together into a beautiful puzzle for the good of everyone! After this trip to Ukraine, belonging to a larger family and having "a tribe" of extended family which spanned the Atlantic Ocean was a treasured gift enjoyed by all of us for many happy years. You can see now more than ever how a sequel could be written to describe further adventures of the "three Didenko sisters turning to five."

It soon became apparent that my father intended this trip to be a personal spiritual journey for him to draw closer to God through making peace with people from his past. A clear pattern developed as he tried to find all his extended family, all his friends even from childhood, and all the work-related acquaintances that he had ever engaged with during his risk laden careers after prison.

In our continued travels, the characters changed, the length of visits varied but the script was ALWAYS the same. For example, when we found his cousin Igor, who was not only his favorite cousin but his best friend from childhood, the reunion that started in early morning lasted well into the night with lots of stories involving both tears and laughter. Other visits, for instance, with an accountant that worked for him in the pine forest, lasted a long afternoon with sweet reminiscing over tea and cookies. However, the script for our many local visits was always the same: reuniting/reconciling with people in his past and drawing closer to God.

We would arrive in the town where we thought the person that my father was looking for lived. We went straight to the train station, which traditionally had the most information about people living in the area. Even when their information was insufficient, we always seemed to still leave with leads to further pursue the quest. We were surprisingly successful in our endeavors. People did not seem to move often, thus supporting my observation that when progress is slow in a country, the values and family mobility follow similar patterns. Children often continue to live in the same town as the second generation, and often even in the same house.

When we would find the house, my father would go knock on the door. After a few of these times, we knew to position ourselves to the side where we could get the best view. As the main door opened, through the screen door, we could see that the person looking a little concerned as they observed a tall man in western clothing and several similarly dressed people to his side.

This was almost predictable, since they were still very fresh coming off the socialist communist system where the natural trained instinct was fear in these situations. After a pause, the concern turned to confusion as they studied my father's face which often caused them to look as if they were seeing a ghost. Then something in their mind would click and they hesitantly would say "Yura, is that you?" as they flung open the door and tried to pull him into a bear hug.

No matter what emotions arose at the time, the script still remained the same. My father would pull away gently, and say, "Stop a moment. It is me and I will not cross your doorstep until I've asked you. Is there anything in our friendship that I would need to ask your forgiveness about, because I have come to do so." There would be another little pregnant pause while his words sank into comprehension. Then with tears in their eyes and shaking their head, they would welcome all of us into their home. After that both parties would go "off script" where ever their hearts took them.

As you would expect, visiting my father's birthplace and the old family estate was a priority stop on our nostalgic journey of revisiting "moments of the past." The day came for that trip to my father's childhood town of Berezan. I felt a strange anticipation as we approached as though being there would somehow tie me closer to my grandfather and his legacy. It seemed that I would more deeply appreciate the Didenko story if I could just walk on the land and touch the soil. It was a beautiful sunny day as we walked the dirt roads and admired the small houses, some still had thatched roofs but all had lush yards with gardens that had both vegetables and flowers growing. My father had known that the big estate house had gone to ruins while he still lived in Ukraine. However, he was surprised to see that it had actually been torn down and a big rectangular factory-like building had been built in its place. But now even that building appeared to be empty and unused. As we walked down the road, I could see my father picturing his childhood and lost in thought. A woman about my age, gardening in her yard, stopped as we passed her house and engaged us in conversation. She was the woman that I mentioned earlier in the book when I described my grandfather's care for his servants who lived on the estate and worked for him.

This woman was now in the third generation of families that lived in the area since my grandfather owned this land. It was touching to hear how her parents passed on the story of stopping neighbors from arguing because they were trampling on Didenko's soul. My father's eyes filled with tears which flashed me back to my after-school visits to the fields on Mrs. Scott 's farm where my father was ploughing with the tractor. The memory filled my own eyes with tears as I quietly whispered to him, "Tato, your father's reputation and the Name of Didenko has finally been vindicated.

The End

Post Script:

On that visit to Beryzan, I filled a little bag of soil and brought it home with me. Seven years later, we buried my father. After they lowered his casket into the ground, I sprinkled that soil all over the top of the closed casket. I know that he was not there, but I know it would make him smile to see his earthly body lying under Ukrainian soil. Even after all these years, I miss you, Tato.

An Invitation to the Reader: *The end of this story can be the beginning of a new journey of hope for you! God has the best plans for your life and has prepared a wonderful home for all who repent, believe in Jesus Christ, and enter a relationship with Him. We invite you to finish here by reading what God who loves you so much has to say about the Lord Jesus Christ and his children in Isaiah 61: 1- 11 **(MN)***

Appendix A

The Journey Home — Timeline and Map

June 1941	Germany invades Russia
Nov 1942	Begin Soviet counter offensive
Feb 1943	Germans surrender in Stalingrad
**Oct 1943	Small wagon train leaves Yasnozir'ya
Nov 1943	Soviets liberate Kiev
**Mar 1944	Sandra is born in a barn on March 24th at about 11:00 pm
**Aug 1944	Entered Czechoslovakia but were trapped in Russian camp
**Mar 1945	Left Czechoslovakia to cross the Austrian foothills
**May 1945	Two wagons arrived at Neu Elm temporary refugee camp and Germany surrenders
**Aug 1945	Train finally departed for Russia with Ukrainians from Neu Elm camp while the Didenko family safely hid in the woods for weeks
**Sep 1945	Moved to Augsburg, Germany refugee camp, Building 4, Room 38 and Japan surrenders ending WWII

**Jan 1949   Boarded a small ship with 69
            Ukrainian passengers to come to the
            United States

**Designates family events among the
historical events of the 2-year Journey

The Didenko Family
2-year Journey

Oct 1943 — Yasnozir'ya — Ukraine

5 months

Limna — Mar 1944

Moldova

5 months

Aug 1944 — Katowice

7 months

Czechia

Slovakia

Hungary

Mar 1945

2 months

May 1945

4 months

Sep 1945 — Augsburg

Austria

Sandra was born in a barn in Limna on March 24, 1944

163

Get to know the authors

Sandra D. Varney, DMD and Moise Ndjomou

Sandra D. Varney, DMD

Sandra Didenko Varney graduated with a bachelor's in chemistry from the University of Rochester; and a DMD from UMDNJ at Rutgers University. She practiced dentistry for 42 years having two consecutive private practices. During that time, she was featured in *Washingtonian* magazine's "Top 100 Dentists in the Metropolitan Area". Dentistry became her life's passion. She always believed in giving back and was very generous toward her patients with her time and often with "gifted" dental work. She volunteered in many community health fairs and N VA Dental Clinic. She did many international dental missions trips, and included her family to actively participate in most of them. Over the years as a family, they touched many lives in countries like Bolivia, Peru, Papua New Guinea, Burkina Faso and Thailand. She lives in Great Falls, VA with her husband, Bob. Their two married daughters and their loving husbands have blessed them with six delightful grandchildren and live nearby. The six "Cuzins" continually bring life, laughter and adventure into their family.

Moise Ndjomou

Moise (Moses) Ndjomou is passionate about God's word and what the Lord does in the nations. He received his Diploma of Advanced Technician in Automotive Mechanics at a young age. After that he worked for a business company in Douala, and also shared the gospel in different places. Later on, he became interested in a formal study of missions. He did his missionary training in Cameroon, India, and the US. He is married to his beautiful and lovely Lisa and together with their children, they serve as missionaries at Youth With A Mission (YWAM) in Togo, West Africa. He earned a Bachelor of Arts in Biblical Studies and was graduated with a Master's in Pioneering Leadership from the University of the Nations (U OF N) in Kona, Hawaii. He has given many courses at U of N schools in multiple countries. Since 2001 Moses has been traveling to different nations to teach God's word and equip young leaders. Moses is fun and loves soccer, laughter, music, and stories.

www.ingramcontent.com/pod-product-compliance
Lightning Source LLC
Chambersburg PA
CBHW060050100426
42742CB00014B/2772